Massee's
Wine Almanac

Massee's Wine Almanac

William E. Massee

Prentice-Hall, Inc., Englewood Cliffs, New Jersey

Massee's Wine Almanac *by William E. Massee*
Copyright © 1980 by William E. Massee

Printed in the United States of America

Prentice-Hall International, Inc. London/Prentice-Hall of Australia, Pty. Ltd., Sydney/Prentice-Hall of Canada, Ltd., Toronto/Prentice-Hall of India Private Ltd., New Delhi/Prentice-Hall of Japan, Inc., Tokyo/Prentice-Hall of Southeast Asia Pte Ltd., Singapore/Whitehall Books Limited, Wellington, New Zealand

10 9 8 7 6 5 4 3 2 1

Library of Congress Cataloging in Publication Data

Massee, William Edman.
  Massee's Wine almanac.

  Includes index.
  1. Wine and wine making. I. Title. II. Title:
Wine almanac.
TP548.M397   641.2'22   80-13391
ISBN 0-13-559658-0
ISBN 0-13-559641-6 (pbk)

Contents

Massee's
Wine Almanac

1.
Vintage Lines: Wines Ready for Drinking 1980-1990

Many great wines can live for a decade and longer—and are drunk too soon. Many good wines begin to fade after five years or so—and are drunk too late.

Good and great wines often cost $10 a bottle and up, and are worth it only when the wines are drunk at their best.

Here are recent vintages of the greatest European regions—Burgundy, Bordeaux, the Rhine, and others. The following key indicates when these wines are likely to be at their best during the 80s.

        Good wines ready.

        Great wines ready. (Good wines holding.)

        Good wines fading. (Great wines holding.)

NOTE: Most wines, of course, are ready to be drunk promptly after bottling, within months of the vintage.

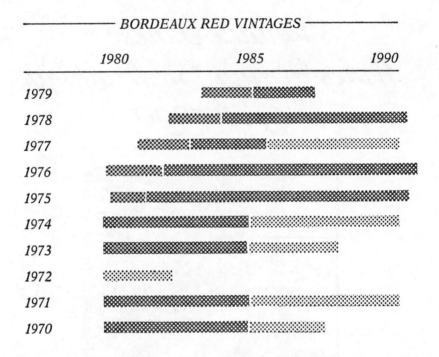

Vintage simply means the harvesting of the grape, and many wines carry the year of the harvest on their labels. A century ago, Port producers, accustomed to blending different years, began bottling wines of exceptional years, "declaring" a vintage; Champagne producers began doing the same.

A vintage year came to signify an exceptional wine and a connoisseur took it upon himself to know all the outstanding vintages. The date on a bottle quickly came to be considered a sign of superiority, and the trade was quick to discover that the public would buy a bottle with a date on it but scorn those without. Today most wines show a year on the label. This practice is to everybody's advantage, for if a shipper blended light wines with full ones, sharp wines with soft ones, he could often produce a better drink than if the various vintages were bottled separately. It should be noted that laws

2

BORDEAUX WHITE VINTAGES

	1980	1985	1990
1979			
1978			
1977			
1976			
1975			
1974*			
1972			
1971			
1970			

*After five years, dry whites begin to decline, even in good years, although sweet wines may continue to be interesting. Vintages not listed are long gone.

regulating wine generally permit a bottle to bear the date of a vintage when at least 75 percent of the wine is from a particular vintage. Since most wines should be drunk before they are four years old, a vintage date serves primarily to indicate the youth of the wine.

The world's best wines are not blends of years. The best wines come from the northern vineyards of France and Germany where frost and cold can limit the crop and lower quality. Bad weather—too hot or too wet—can harm a vintage anywhere but improved methods of tending vines and making wines minimize negative conditions. Many good wines at reasonable prices now come from new regions and those once ignored—California, New York, Oregon and Washington, among others.

————————— *BURGUNDY RED VINTAGES* —————————

	1980	1985	1990

1979

1978

1977

1976

1975

1974

1973

1972

1971

1970

————————— *BURGUNDY WHITE VINTAGES* —————————

	1980	1985	1990

1979

1978

1977

1976

1975

1974

1973

1971

4

RHÔNE VINTAGES

	1980	1985	1990
1979	░░░░░░░░ ▓▓▓▓▓▓▓▓ ░░░		
1978	░░░ ▓▓▓▓▓▓ ░░░		
1977	▓▓▓▓▓▓▓▓ ░░░░░░░░░░░		
1976	▓▓▓ ░░░░░░		
1975	░░░░░░░░		
1974	░░░░░░░░		
1973	░░		
1972	▓▓ ░░░░░		
1971	▓▓▓▓▓ ░░░░░░░		
1970	▓▓▓ ░░░░░░░		

LOIRE VINTAGES

	1980	1985	1990
1979	░░ ▓▓▓▓▓▓ ░░░		
1978	▓▓▓▓▓ ░░░		
1977	░░░░░		
1976	░░░░░░░		
1975	░░░		

▓▓▓ Good wines ready.
▓▓▓ Great wines ready. (Good wines holding.)
░░░ Good wines fading. (Great wines holding.)

———————————— *ALSACE VINTAGES* ————————————

	1980	1985	1990
1979			
1978			
1977			
1976			
1975			

———————————— *RHINE AND MOSELLE VINTAGES* ————————————

	1980	1985	1990
1979			
1978			
1977			
1976			
1975			
1974			
1973			
1972			
1971			
1970			

———————————— *ITALIAN VINTAGES* ————————————

	1980	*1985*	*1990*
1979		▓▓▓▓▓▓ ▓▓▓▓▓▓▓▓	
1978	▓▓▓▓ ▓▓▓▓▓▓▓▓▓▓▓▓▓▓▓▓ ░░░░░		
1977	▓▓▓▓▓▓ ▓▓▓▓▓▓▓▓▓▓▓▓ ░░░░░░░		
1975	▓▓▓▓▓▓▓▓▓▓▓▓▓▓▓▓▓ ░░░░░░░		
1974	▓▓▓▓▓▓▓▓▓▓▓▓ ░░░░░░░░░░░░░░		
1973	░░░░░░░░░░░		
1971	▓▓▓▓▓▓▓▓▓▓▓▓▓▓▓ ░░░░░░░░░░░░░░░░░░░░░░░░		
1970	░░░░░░░░░░░░░░░░░░░		

Even in northern vineyards of France and Germany, vintage ratings are of less importance than they were a decade ago. Laboratories in every region check the maturing grapes and the developing wines to stop trouble before it begins. As the technology of grape growing and wine making generally gets better, vintages have less significance.

A large and good vintage at reasonable prices means more to most of us than a small but costly vintage of superior wines. The year on a bottle helps us find the big vintages. The main value of a vintage date, though, is to lead us to young wines and help us avoid those that may be too old.

At one time only three or four years in a decade produced good wines, but now awareness of what goes on in vine and vat enables producers to offer floods of good wine almost every other year.

Vintages are important on old wines made in the days when fermentation was allowed to go on longer. Wines were stored two years or more in casks so that they would last for decades. Many red wines are fermented today in less than ten

7

days, whereas most white wines are not matured at all in wood; thus wines are ready sooner than they were. Wines have a shorter life span today—most less than ten years— because of the shorter fermentation period. Winegrowers simply cannot afford to tie up their money in stored wines for extended periods of time. A few good wines are still made in the old way—Sauternes, Champagne, Port—but these are all expensive.

Vintages still do make a difference—within individual districts. One man will delay the picking of grapes for a few days to build up sugar in the grape; fermentation will be extended for a few hours; wines will be left a little longer in the wood; bottled wines will be held until they develop. Distinctions remain, dependent more on people than on weather. The vintage date may lead you to such wines. But only your taste can tell.

2.
Vintage Ratings and Rankings 1970-1979

Vintage Ratings are customarily based on a scale from 1 to 20. The wines are valued at their worth when the decade began and not when the wines were made:

    20–18 Outstanding wines

    17–15 Many great wines, many good wines

    14–12 Some good wines, many only fair

    11 or less A few fair wines, mostly poor wines

NOTE: Good vineyards—and good winemakers—produce exceptions to the rule. Non-vintage wines, as well as blends of vintages, can be best buys.

Big vintages can mean low prices. The Seventies saw some of the biggest vintages on record; many of the wines are now prime for drinking through the Eighties:
    1979, 1978, 1976, 1973, 1970
Great vintages—*those that produce excellent long-lived wines, are often small and high in price. Wines are lowest in price when they first come on the market, but then you may have to wait five years or so to drink them. These are the great vintages of the Seventies:*
    Bordeaux: 1976, 1975, 1971, 1970
    Burgundy: 1976, 1972, 1971, 1970
    Rhineland: 1976, 1975, 1973, 1971
    Northern Italy: 1975, 1974, 1971, 1970

BORDEAUX VINTAGES

The best vineyards of Bordeaux have the words "Grand Cru Classé" on their labels and may take ten years to develop. Those called collectively *Petits Châteaux* may develop in four years, as do those with district names like Saint Emilion, Pomerol, Graves, and Médoc. Those from Haut Médoc townships—Margaux, Saint Julien, Pauillac, and Saint Estèphe—take as long. Bordeaux Rouge and Bordeaux Supérieur and the white wines are drinkable three years after the vintage. Lists for all of these start on page 56.

Red Bordeaux

1979 Good quantity, good wines. *13–15*
    1978 Excellent wines from a crop slightly smaller than average. A cold summer with little rainfall and a warm

dry fall produced grapes with a concentration of sugar and somewhat high acid. The wines will live long and are already high in price. Similar to 1966. *16–19*

1977 A small vintage, hampered by spring frosts that reduced quantities of softening Merlot. Balanced wines somewhat light, but long-lived. Played down at first compared with touted 1976 and 1975, the wines are lower in price, many offering good value. *14–17*

1976 From a large crop after a hot summer and autumn rains, the light and fruity wines have a rich, lingering taste. Already drinkable, the wines will be delightful all through the decade. *16–19*

1975 A small crop of intense wines perhaps lacking in fruit. Wines for the Nineties, with Saint Emilions and *Petits Châteaux* reaching their peaks during the last half of the decade. *15–17*

1974 Rains in late summer and early fall made for a dull wine, balanced but without much charm. Pleasant for drinking in the last half of the decade. *13–15*

1973 A record crop of light wines, for drinking during the first half of the Eighties. Prices at first were low, and there may still be bargains in the market from importers who bought early. *15–17*

1972 A late harvest, and a small one, of thin wines, hard and acid—a green year. Austere wines now well developed, illustrating what good winemaking practices can do for a mediocre vintage. For drinking in the first half of the Eighties. *10–12*

1971 A small crop, with little Merlot to soften the Cabernet because of a cold spring, but the wines developed quickly, being light. Now have great elegance and marvelous balance and are expected to hold for a long time, into the Nineties. *15–18*

1970 An enormous crop of big, rounded wines easy to drink. Attractive wines for drinking all through the Eighties. *16–19*

It is said that the French drink Bordeaux too young, the English drink clarets too old, and Americans drink them when they get them. The wines come on the market some three years after the vintage and the French drink them before the decade is out, whereas the English prefer clarets when they are well into their second decade. Pomerols and Saint Emilions, with much Merlot and Cabernet Franc, can be delicious five years after the vintage, but they become much more subtle after ten years. Wines from top vineyards and touted vintages only begin to be developed after a decade and many a bottle is glorious when it is thirty years old. The problem is one of storage; a wine subject to temperature changes and vibration gets old before its time. For those who can keep a wine steady, somewhere below 60°F, here are some older vintages that deserve good storage:

——————————— *Old Bordeaux Vintages* ———————————

	1980	*1985*	*1990*
1969	▓▓▓▓▓▓▓▓▓▓▓		
1967	▓▓▓▓▓▓▓▓		
1966	██████████▓▓▓	▓▓▓▓▓▓▓▓▓	
1964	▓▓▓▓▓		
1962	█████▓▓▓▓▓	▓▓▓▓▓▓▓▓▓▓	
1961	████████████████████████████		
1959	▓▓▓▓▓▓▓▓▓▓▓▓▓▓		

Great wines ready. Good wines holding. ████████████
Great wines holding. Good wines fading. ▓▓▓▓▓▓▓▓

————————— *White Bordeaux* —————————

The dry whites of Graves and others from Entre-Deux-Mers, or those called Blanc de Blancs, are harvested at about the same time as the reds and have similar vintage ratings. The *sweet* wines of Sauternes and Barsac and minor districts are harvested later, when rain or frost can damage the grapes.

The dry wines fade after four years or so, but the sweet wines only begin to develop in that time and are at their best during their second decade. Here are the recent vintages for Sauternes and other *sweet* wines:

1979 Good quantity, good wines. *13–15*

1978 A small crop, nearly a third below average, of excellent wines, elegant but not rich. *16–18*

1977 Disaster.

1976 Harvest rains damaged the vintage. *12–14*

1975 Marvelous, rich wines from a small crop. *18–20*

1974 Disaster.

1973 An enormous crop of wines on the light side. *14–18*

1972 Disaster.

1971 A small crop of superb wines. *18–20*

1970 A large crop of luscious, elegant wines. *18–20*

————————— *BURGUNDY VINTAGES* —————————

Reds from Grand Cru and Premier Cru vineyards may take four years to mature, whites are ready in three years, and most are past their best when ten years old. Only the greatest growths in great years continue into their second decade. Wines bearing township names are drinkable in three years, whereas southern Burgundies like Mâcon Blanc or Mâcon

Rouge are ready in two years; most Beaujolais is best when less than a year old.

Most Burgundies are chaptalized (sugar is added to the must, or juice of the grapes) to increase alcohol to 12 percent or more. Demand encourages growers to get maximum yields. These wines, high in alcohol and high in price, often begin to fade after five years. Large vineyards are broken up with several owners, some doing their own bottling, others selling to brokers. Estate bottlings, that is, wines made by the owners, are identified on the label with phrases like *Mise en bouteille au Domaine*, with the name of the grower as *Propriétaire*, *Récoltant*, or *Viticulteur*. These are preferred by the experts in the hope that pride has encouraged the owners to produce the best possible wines. Wines from shippers are labeled *Négociant-Eleveur*; many of these are excellent as well. Lists begin on page 39.

———————————— *Red Burgundy* ————————————

Wines from the divided vineyards vary with the winemaker so it is more important to make the selection of wines based on a particular vintage or producer than to make a choice based on the vineyard.

1979 Good quantity of typical wines. *13–15*

1978 Average crop of full-bodied wines. High in price. *16–18*

Enormous crop of Beaujolais. Light wines for prompt drinking. *13–16*

1977 Small crop of good wines. *15–17*

Poor Beaujolais, now passé.

1976 A large crop of fabulous, full-bodied, balanced wines for drinking through the Eighties. *17–19*

Fruity, splendid Beaujolais, but past their prime.

1975 A disaster.

1974 Fall rains limited the crop, producing some fruity, distinctive wines, now almost gone. *13–14*

1973 Large crop of light wines with fine bouquet, now almost gone. *15–17*

1972 Large crop of full-bodied wines, now almost gone. *16–18*

1971 Small crop of intense, full wines going fast. *16–19*

1970 Large crop of light, delicious wines, almost gone. *15–16*

―――――――――――― *White Burgundy* ――――――――――――

All but the greatest dry whites of Burgundy should probably be drunk before they are five years old, even the greatest scarcely staying at their prime after ten years. Even so, when the top whites are kept in cool cellars, they can be rewarding after twenty years, offering an intensity and compelling steeliness of taste that is astounding; more often, though, the old wines simply fall apart.

1979 Good quantity of typical wines. *13–16*

1978 Small crop of good wines high in price. *15–16*

1977 Small crop, with few good wines. *12–13*

1976 Large crop of full, rich wines for drinking in the early Eighties. *17–19*

1975 Full wines, to be drunk up. *14–15*

1974 Large crop of light, distinguished wines, now almost gone. *13–14*

1973 Large crop of elegant wines for drinking in the early Eighties, but costly. *16–17*

1972 Average crop of hard wines, now almost gone. *10*

1971 Small crop. A few full, intense wines, going fast. *12–13*

1970 Large crop of light wines, now gone. .

————————— *RHÔNE VINTAGES* —————————

Vineyards cluster along Rhône slopes below Lyon, running on down into Provence, producing freshets of Côtes-du-Rhône, mostly red and rosé, among the best buys of all French wines. Vintages can be said to follow Burgundian patterns, yet their southerly aspects protect them from frost, and only occasional wet spells harm usually abundant crops. Modern methods minimize such problems. Villages produce wines so distinctive that they warrant adding their names to the regional label, districts being elevated to VDQS (see pp. 74-75) status and then to *Appellation Contrôlée* as the wines improve.

    Most of the wines are drinkable when they come on the market, but districts like Hermitage, Crozes-Hermitage, Côte Rôtie, and Châteauneuf-du-Pape continue to improve into their second decade. Côtes-du-Rhône Nouveau, full and fruity, patterned after Beaujolais, is finding enthusiasts, as do all the Rhônes, particularly when regional Burgundy and Bordeaux climb above the five dollar mark.

    1979 Good quantity, very good wines. *15–17*

    1978 Large crop of excellent wines, full-bodied and fruity. *17–19*

    1977 Late crop, smaller than average, of good, light wines. *16–17*

    1976 Large crop of well-developed wines, helped by a hot summer. *16–18*

    1975 Below average crop of mediocre wines because of rainy weather. *12–13*

    1974 Poor wines.

    1973 Huge crop of ordinary wines, but good wines from northern regions, such as Hermitage. *13–15*

    1972 Average crop of big, long-lived wines. *15–16*

    1971 Small crop and rainy vintage, with some fine wines from top vineyards. *16–17*

    1970 Large crop of superior wines, full and generous. *17–19*

—————— *Older Rhône Vintages* ——————

Northern districts of the Rhône, below Lyon, produce full-bodied, long-lived wines from Hermitage and Côte Rôtie, and many good bottles from the 1969 vintage still rate 16–17, excellent drinking during the Eighties. Good earlier vintages like 1966 and 1967 now rank somewhat lower and are beginning to fade.

Southern districts like Châteauneuf-du-Pape produce wines that approach their prime when five years old and may have faded when they are ten. Rosés of Tavel and Lirac are best as soon as they are bottled, within two years of the vintage.

—————— *LOIRE VINTAGES* ——————

Dry wines from districts along the Loire are best drunk young, as soon as they are bottled, within two or three years of the vintage. Sweet wines are made in good years at Vouvray in the Touraine and in districts of the Anjou, particularly Quarts de Chaume and Bonnezeaux; these rank with the best sweet wines of the world and can live for a decade and longer.

1979 Good quantity, good wines.

1978 Small crop, some good wines.

1977 Short crop of thin wines, now mostly gone.

NOTE: Outstanding years for sweet wines were 1976, 1973, and 1971.

————————— *CHAMPAGNE VINTAGES* —————————

Best buys in Champagne are blends of different years called *cuvées*, marketed as *Brut* (extremely dry), *Extra Sec* (dry), and *Sec* (dryish). Exceptional vintages are bottled when the crop warrants, usually coming on the market six years after the vintage; they command premium prices. Champagnes can be drunk as soon as they appear on the market, rarely warranting holding more than a few months.
Exceptional vintages *1976, 1975, 1973, 1971, 1970.*

————————— *ALSATIAN VINTAGES* —————————

Excellent white wines from Rhineland grapes—Riesling, Gewürztraminer, Sylvaner—are made in Alsace; these are often drier and less elegant than those to the north, from the Rheingau and Moselle. Most are meant to be drunk young, within two or three years of the vintage, although those picked late in the vintage can be as fruity as their German counterparts and can last a decade. Sylvaner was the familiar white wine of France not so long ago, the white counterpart of Beaujolais or Côtes-du-Rhône, but rising prices have turned French affections to Muscadet and Mâcon Blanc, with growing attention being paid to Entre-Deux-Mers from Bordeaux. Unlike German wines, mostly drunk by themselves, those from Alsace are intended to be drunk with meals.
1979 Good quantity, good wines.
1978 Fair crop of good wines.
1977 Above average crop of good light wines.
1976 Abundant crop of full, fruity wines.
1975 Large crop of fruity, elegant wines.

NOTE: Wines from grapes picked late, fruity and sweet, may still be found from good vintages of 1974, 1973, and 1971. Vintages generally follow German patterns.

ITALIAN VINTAGES

As with most Mediterranean vineyards, and those of California, vintages are generally good, provided frosts do not harm the flowering in spring, thus reducing quantity, and provided bad weather during harvest does not harm the grapes, which lowers quality. Dry weather produces intense wines, wet summers produce light wines or rot grapes, but modern practices generally produce good wines. Vineyards in the Alpine foothills of Piedmont and Lombardy and north of Venice have somewhat harsher climates that stress the vines, producing better wines, as do the microclimates of California's coastal ranges.

Even so, some vintages are better than others.

1979 Good quantity, good to very good wines.
1978 Below average crop of excellent wines.
1977 Small crop of good wines in Tuscany, generally poor elsewhere.
1976 Poor wines.
1975 Good Chiantis, generally poor elsewhere.
1974 Large crop of excellent wines.
1973 Some good wines.
1972 Poor wines.
1971 Large crop of many good wines.
1970 Large crop of many good wines.

---------------------- GERMAN VINTAGES ----------------------

There used to be 25,000 vineyards in Germany, causing such confusion that it was decreed that none should be smaller than a dozen acres. Small plots were united into big vineyards, or *Grosslagen*, reducing the number to 2,500, and regions were divided into districts, or *Bereichen*. Most of the wine exported is identified on the label either by *Grosslage* or *Bereiche*, while most of the famous vineyards were large enough to keep their names.

The wines were also graded: Tafelwein is an ordinary blend drunk locally and not worth exporting; Qualitätswein is a blend of wine from a particular region; such wine is often identified as QbA (for *Qualitätswein bestimmter Anbaugebiete*—quality wine from designated regions), inexpensive and often good. The fermenting juice is sugared to bring the resulting wine up to 10 or 11 percent alcohol, in the common French practice called chaptalization.

Wines made only with natural sugar in the grape are called *Qualitätswein mit Prädikat* and are the best. *Kabinett* is the driest grade, flowery and elegant. *Spätlese*, from late-picked grapes, is more flowery; *Auslese*, from selected bunches, is fruity and lightly sweet. Wine made from over-ripe bunches, *Beerenauslese*, and from sorting out dried grapes, *Trockenbeerenauslese*, are progressively sweeter, rarer, and costlier. For those who seek glorious wines not compellingly rich, the single word to look for on a German label is *Kabinett*.

—————————— *Rhine and Moselle* ——————————

1979 Good quantity, very good wines.

1978 Latest vintage in memory, the crop a third below normal on the Rhine, two-thirds below normal in the Moselle. Some Kabinett wines, some QbA.

1977 Average crop of dry, fruity wines; much QbA.

1976 Below average crop, but much hot weather produced outstanding wines, much Auslese and Spätlese and sweeter wines, rich and luscious. Best of the decade.

1975 Superb, balanced Moselles, particularly Kabinett; some good Rhines, a few Kabinett.

1974 Small crop of thin wines.

1973 Enormous crop of many excellent wines, all grades.

1972 Thin wines.

1971 Small crop of outstanding wines of Kabinett grade and better, compared to 1959 and 1953. Prädikat wines rich and balanced.

1970 Large crop of light, dry wines, now fading.

Wine is a tranquilizer, Burgundy more than Bordeaux.
Wine reduces emotional tension.
Wine is a food and a drug.
Wine is the milk of old age. (Quotation from Osler.)
Even two ounces of wine make people feel better.
Wine has low sodium content, high potassium content.
(From extracts of a medical symposium on health benefits of wine.)

─────────── *CALIFORNIA VINTAGES* ───────────

Microclimates in the coastal ranges are affected by frost, wet, and drought, but superb vine tending and winemaking—and the desire to excel—produce fine wines every year, minimizing the importance of vintages. There is a California style: big wines made to bring out the fruit of the grape, seeming exaggerations of European styles. The wines develop more rapidly, in general, and there is a belief that they decline more rapidly than their European peers, although the new plantings of supervines in the Seventies and before have scarcely had time to show staying powers. Listed below are the top varieties in the vineyards and vintage lines showing when the 1979 vintages should be ready to drink:

─────────────── *Reds 1979* ───────────────

	1980	1985	1990	Original European areas
Cabernet Sauvignon		▓▓▓▓▓▓	▓▓▓▓▓▓▓	Bordeaux
Merlot		▓▓ ▓▓▓▓▓	▓▓▓▓▓▓	Bordeaux
Pinot Noir		▓▓▓▓▓▓▓▓▓	░░	Burgundy
Gamay Beaujolais	▓		▓▓▓▓▓	Burgundy
Petite Sirah		▓▓ ▓▓▓▓	░░	Rhône
Zinfandel		▓▓▓▓▓ ▓▓▓▓▓▓	▓	Yugoslavia
Gamay Noir	▓▓▓▓▓	▓▓▓▓ ░░░		Beaujolais
Barbera	▓▓	▓▓▓▓ ░░		Italy
Garignane	▓▓	▓▓▓▓▓ ░░		Rhône

22

──────────── *Whites 1979* ────────────

	1980	1985	1990	
Chardonnay (or Pinot Chardonnay)	░░░░░░░░░░░░			Burgundy
Sauvignon Blanc (or Fumé Blanc)	░░░░░░░░			Bordeaux, Upper Loire
White Riesling (or Johannisberg Riesling)	░░░░░░░░░░░░			Rhine
Chenin Blanc	░░░░░░░░░░░░			Middle Loire
Pinot Blanc	░░░░░░░░░░░░░░░░░			Southern Burgundy
Gewürztraminer	░░░░░░			Alsace
Sylvaner	░░░░░░░░			Alsace, Rhine

NOTE: *White wines from late-harvest grapes, gratifyingly sweet, easily last a decade. Cabernet Sauvignon and Merlot also last ten years or longer. Pinot Noir, Zinfandel, and Petite Sirah often fade after seven or eight years, although many of them continue excellent into their second decade.*

3.
Buying

―――― *GOOD CHEAP WINES FOR THE EIGHTIES* ――――

Wines that cost under $3 when the Seventies began were
higher by mid-decade, reaching $4 to $6 by its end. Those
who had learned to love Chianti and Soave, Beaujolais and
Muscadet, rebelled. They switched to jug wines.

Then a flood of new $3 wines came in: Rioja from
Spain, VDQS from France, some from Eastern Europe, South
America. Just as people got to know them, inflation jogged
prices. Back to jugs.

Anybody accustomed to buying brands—package
goods in supermarkets, quality items in specialty shops—is
confused by the wide range of prices in liquor stores and wary
of the strange names, particularly new ones. Just what is the
brand? The name of a region like Burgundy or Chianti isn't a

brand. How about the name of the exporter, like Chanson or B & G? Or the name of the importer, like Monsieur Henri or Austin Nichols? Surely a vineyard name is a brand, like Château Lafite, but Burgundy vineyards have several owners, so each owner's name becomes a brand. Brand names with big budgets now command the market, a quartet of blends accounting for almost 80 percent of imports. Many are priced below $4, some above:

> Liebfraumilch from the Rhineland
> > (Blue Nun, Madrigal, and 40 more)
> Lambrusco from Italy
> > (Riunite, Ruffino, and a score more)
> Sangria from Spain
> > (Yago, Real, and a dozen more)
> Rosé from Portugal
> > (Mateus, Lancer's, and half a dozen more)

As for dry table wines, Mouton Cadet and Marquisat may be familiar, as may be producers whose names on a line of wines are recognized. Ginestet or Calvet in Bordeaux, Patriarche or Bichot in Burgundy, Sichel or Deinhard in Germany, Bolla or Antinori in Italy, Almadén or Paul Masson in California—all are more or less familiar. Most of their brands are $4 and up.

All the confusion is good news for wine buyers. Just look for bottles priced around $3. New wines are introduced at low prices to seduce purchasers.

The trick is to try any new wines on the market, no matter what the country, region, producer, importer, or even brand, and when you find a wine you like, buy a case or more before the price goes up. Wise buyers get a mixed case of the new wines every season, stocking a case or two for everyday drinking. They average about $30 a case. The glory of wine is its variety, and the unknown can be wonderful.

At least a score of countries are trying to establish themselves on the American market. Here are some wines to look for. Personal favorites include wines from Portugal and Chile, but others should not be overlooked.

● *Portugal* Vinho Verde is the generic name for fresh young reds and whites from the north, but also look for Dāo and Colares.

● *Austria* Many fresh, dryish young whites with grape names from Wachau (up the Danube), Vienna's suburb of Grinzing, Gumpoldskirchener, Neusiedlersee.

● *Hungary* Full, dry reds from Kadarka and other grapes, whites from Furmint, Harzlevelü.

● *Yugoslavia* Adriatica is main export brand; reds dry, whites often soft.

● *Romania* Premiat is export brand. Look for Cabernet Sauvignon.

● *Greece* Look for dry reds from exporters like Achaia-Clauss, Cambas.

● *Israel* Carmel is export brand. Look for Cabernet Sauvignon and Sauvignon Blanc.

● *Algeria* Having difficulty breaking into market, but look for reds, many designated VDQS when country was part of France.

● *Argentina* Enormous production, but look for reds from European vines, from exporters like Toso, Valmont, or Trappiche.

● *Chile* Experiencing export problems, but many fine wines from European varieties, particularly those ranked *Gran Vino* or *Reservado* from exporters like Undurraga, Licores Mitjan, Valdivieso.

Countries that have shipped wines here for generations are now exporting wines from little-known regions, as well as new types. Often these are of excellent quality because of modern vine-tending and winemaking methods. Many vineyards have been replanted in noble vines and the wines are some of the best buys available:

● *Spain* Many Riojas are still reasonably priced, not only dry, rounded *Reservas*, but also the fresh, light reds called Clarete. Look for Valdepeñas and the lesser Manchego, other reds from Panadés or Toro, whites from Alella and Ribiera. Don't miss dry Sherries like Manzanilla and Fino, or Montilla.

● *France* Many still reasonably priced Côtes-du-Rhône bottlings are being shipped. There are excellent Saint Emilion and *Petits Châteaux* reds from Bordeaux, many dry whites from Entre-Deux-Mers. Some of Burgundy's Mâcon Blanc is still reasonable, as are bottlings from various places called Blanc de Blancs. See detailed lists for each region and take particular note of VDQS listings, page 74.

● *Germany* Rating systems established during the Seventies have established QbA, from a *Bereich* (region) or *Grosslage* (large combined vineyard), as a grade of wine to look for. See lists for Germany. Wines from Baden and the Bergstrasse, Frankenwein from Franconia, and bottlings from the Nahe are beginning to appear. The fragrant, often-soft bottlings can be superb values.

● *Italy* New rating systems and government encouragement of the wine industry have widened the range of Italian wines available at reasonable prices, including whites from vineyards north of Venice, in the Veneto, Alto Adige, and Friuli; Tuscan reds other than Chianti; reds and whites from Sicily and elsewhere. All are worth looking for. See Italian listings.

NOTE: Tastes of strange wines can be surprising and you may have to drink several glasses before deciding what is best with them. Soft whites generally taste best by themselves or with light, spicy, or salty dishes. Sharp whites, which are rare, may taste best with smoked foods or those with pronounced tastes. Sharp reds and fruity young ones may taste best with hearty stews or pasta dishes. Full reds may taste best with roasts or barbecued meats. Wines too light may need a squeeze of lemon, those too full a spritz of soda; ice may be called for; or the wines may be blended. Those with brand names are sometimes bland and sweetish, made to appeal to a wide audience. They can often be adjusted with lemon, soda, and ice.

———— HOW TO BUY TEN OF THE MOST ————
POPULAR DRY WINES

Offered in a range of quality, and price, each of these wines can be found in most stores and on most wine lists.

——————————— Whites ———————————

    •*Chablis* The epitome of light, dry elegance—and the wine most imitated—Chablis should be drunk within two years of the vintage; some 250,000 cases are made in a good year. Petit Chablis, like Beaujolais, is drunk within the year, mostly in carafe; there are some 50,000 cases. Grand Cru (some 20,000 cases) and Premier Cru (perhaps 140,000 cases) are best drunk before three years old. They are the lightest wines made from the Chardonnay grape, and the driest. *Alternatives*: Fruitier Montagny or Rully from Burgundy's Chalonnais, fuller Saint Véran and Mâcon Blanc from southern Burgundy, or those called Chardonnay or Pinot Chardonnay from Chile, New York, or elsewhere. Chardonnay from California is usually full and fruity, more like white Burgundies of the Côte d'Or.

    •*Pouilly-Fuissé* Overpriced. Light and fruity but fuller than Chablis, best before three years old; some 300,000 cases are produced. *Alternatives*: Pouilly-Vinzelles, Pouilly-Loché, and Saint Véran may be less in price. Also try the alternatives listed under Blanc de Blancs and Chablis.

    •*Muscadet* Once considered a carafe wine, this dry and fruity Loire has become fashionable in Paris. Some 6 million

cases are produced, Muscadet de Sèvre-et-Main being preferred to Muscadet des Côteaux de la Loire or just plain
Muscadet. Muscadet-sur-lie is considered to have a more
pronounced taste, while that made from Gros Plant (the
grape called Folle Blanche elsewhere) may be drier. All
should be drunk young, when perhaps two years old. *Alternatives*: Similar wines made elsewhere are less tart. Perhaps
Blanc de Blancs or Entre-Deux-Mers from Bordeaux, but
these are made from different grapes.

●*Soave* Italy's best-known white wine, dry and light,
but soft. Often ordinary in large blends of big shippers, small
growers and the cooperative *Cantina Sociale* offer wines of
remarkable fruitiness and freshness. Best drunk when less
than three years old. *Alternatives*: Soave is generally softer
than other whites priced competitively. Try Sylvaner.

●*Riesling* Flowery, light, and distinctive, the grape that
produces all the great Rhine wines, the best of which are
made to be sweet. Fresh, dry versions from Moselle and Rhine
districts are marketed as QbA or Kabinett, from a *Bereich*
(region) or a *Grosslage* (large combined vineyard). Best when
less than three years old. *Alternatives*: Riesling from Alsace,
Austria, and elsewhere. In California, where they are called
White Riesling or Johannisberg Riesling, the wines are different, lighter and fruitier, closer in style to sweet Spätlesen
and Auslesen. Similar wines from Riesling crosses (Müller-
Thurgau, particularly) in Franconia, Baden, and elsewhere
are somewhat less distinguished but cheaper.

———————————————— *Reds* ————————————————

●*Beaujolais* The epitome of fresh, fruity young wine.
Some 4 million cases of Beaujolais and Beaujolais Supérieur
are produced in a good year, meant to be drunk promptly,
preferably from cask or carafe. Beaujolais-Villages (2 million
cases) is a better grade, to be drunk up before the following

vintage. Even the nine Beaujolais Crus (growths) are best drunk within the year, although Moulin-à-Vent and Morgon are considered to improve after a year or so in bottle. Chiroubles and Saint-Amour, Fleurie and Juliénas, Brouilly and Côte de Brouilly, and Chénas are best drunk young as possible. Beaujolais Nouveau, hastily vinified to reach Paris early in November, is often harsh. Similar Beaujolais Primeur, perhaps longer fermented, tastes the same. Beaujolais de l'Année, usually available after the first of the year, is the customary fermentation, meant to be drunk before the next vintage. *Alternatives*: There's nothing like Beaujolais, but Nouveau wines being made on the Rhône, in California, and elsewhere are often worth trying.

●*Châteauneuf-du-Pape* Overpriced. This full, fruity wine of the lower Rhône, soft and easy to drink three years after the vintage and good for perhaps five years more, is the most popular of all Rhônes, demand exceeding the more than 2 million cases produced each year. *Alternatives*: Côtes-du-Rhône, Piedmont reds. Hermitage and Côte Rôtie, often lower in price, are superior.

●*Chianti* The most popular of all Italian wines, the best of the million cases made each year are considered to be from four areas: Chianti Classico, Rufina, Montalbano, and Colli Fiorentini. Those called Riservas are aged three years, full and fruity wines with a clean, dry taste. Young Chiantis have a prickly, pleasing quality because some wine made from raisinized grapes is added to the regular fermentation, a process called *governo*. Most of the wine is shipped in regular bottles these days, the straw-covered ones now being expensive to make.

●*Valpolicella*, *Bardolino* Practically twins, and generally spoken of in the same breath, both are from vineyards near Verona, both light and fruity and best two or three years after the vintage. Valpolicella is considered somewhat fuller and better. Bardolino can be drunk within a year of the vintage, a delightful rival to Beaujolais. Both market grades called Superiore, aged a year or longer in wood, and are worth seeking.

NOBLE VINES

Of all the things there are to learn about wine, by far the most important are the names of the grapes that produce the best bottles. Knowing them, you can take part in wine talk, which is boring, you can learn the names of vineyards where the vines grow, which is confusing, or you can begin tasting the wines. The tastings will be even more confusing, but they won't be boring.

You might start with white wines. Chardonnay produces the best dry white wines—from it comes all the great white Burgundy—but try those of California. Compare wine price for price.

Riesling produces all the great Rhine wines. See how they vary from light Moselles to full Rheingaus. Or taste the range of sweetness, from Kabinett through the Auslesen.

Or taste the range of red wines from Bordeaux, contrasting them with Cabernet Sauvignon from California.

Knowing the grapes, you get to know the wines.

TEN BEST WINE GRAPES (RED)

Grapevine	Best Locations
Pinot Noir	Burgundy; California; Champagne; Italy; Middle Europe.
Cabernet Sauvignon	Bordeaux, especially Médoc and Graves; California; Middle Europe; Chile; elsewhere.

Cabernet Franc	*Bordeaux, especially Saint Emilion; Middle Loire (reds like Champigny, Chinon, Saint Nicolas, and Bourgueil; rosés); Chile.*
Merlot	*Bordeaux, especially Pomerol; California; Italy.*
Nebbiolo	*Italy, especially Piedmont and Lombardy. Also known as Spanna.*
Syrah	*Rhône; especially Hermitage.*
Malbec	*Bordeaux; Cahors. Also known as Cot or Pressac.*
Gamay	*Beaujolais, where it is known as Gamay Noir à Jus Blanc. Many varieties. Gamay Noir was once called Napa Gamay in California, where the grape called Gamay Beaujolais has been identified as a Pinot Noir.*
San Giovese	*Italy, especially Chianti. Also known as San Gioveto.*
Grenache	*Southern Italy; northern Spain; California, particularly for rosé. Also known as Ganarcha.*

NOTE: Of the hundreds of red wine grapes, two minor European varieties have produced remarkable wines in California. Zinfandel has been identified as the Plavac of Yugoslavia and the Primitivo of southern Italy. Petite Sirah is probably descended from the Duriff of the Rhône. Cabernet hybrids are widely planted in California, particularly Ruby Cabernet, while New York does well with French crosses like Baco Noir and Maréchal Foch, Chelois and de Chaunac, Chancellor and Léon Millot.

——————— *TWELVE BEST WINE GRAPES (WHITE)* ———————

Grapevine	Best Locations
Chardonnay	Burgundy; California; Pacific Northwest; Champagne. Also known as Pinot Chardonnay.
Sauvignon Blanc	Upper Loire; Bordeaux; California; Pacific Northwest. Also known as Blanc Fumé, Fumé Blanc.
Riesling	Rhineland; Alsace; Middle Europe; Pacific Northwest; California. Also known as White Riesling, Johannisberg Riesling.
Gewürtzraminer	Alsace; Rhineland; California; Pacific Northwest; Italy. Also known as Traminer.
Pinot Blanc	Lesser Burgundy vineyards; California.
Chenin Blanc	Middle Loire; California. Also known as Pineau de la Loire.
Folle Blanche	Lower Loire; California. Also known as Gros Plant, Picpoul.
Sémillon	Bordeaux; Monbazillac; California. Used with Sauvignon Blanc to produce dry Graves, sweet Sauternes and Barsac.
Sylvaner	Rhineland; Franconia; Alsace; Middle Europe; Tyrol; California. Also known as Franken Riesling and (in California) Riesling.
Viognier	Rhône.

Trebbiano	*Italy; Provence, California. Also known as Ugni Blanc and (in Cognac) Saint Emilion.*
Pinot Grigio	*Italy; Alsace; Baden. Also known as Tokay d'Alsace and Rülander.*

NOTE: Like the last two grapes, which excel in Italy, there are also Verdiso and Verdicchio, Vermentino and Cortese, not much tried outside Italy. Also, Riesling hybrids like Müller-Thurgau, Scheurebe, and Kerner, now extensively planted in Germany, deserve more attention.

——— THE GEOGRAPHY OF THE WORLD'S ——— GREATEST WINES

Wines are known by the places they come from—the region, the district, the township or commune, and finally, the vineyard. The more specific the name, the better the wine. Listed below are outstanding vineyards from the top townships in the major districts of the three greatest wine regions: Bordeaux, Burgundy, and the Rhineland:

——————————— BORDEAUX ———————————

Médoc	Margaux—*Château Margaux* Saint Julien—*Château Léoville-Poyferré* Pauillac—*Château Lafite, Château Latour, Château Mouton-Rothschild* Saint Estèphe—*Château Cos d'Estournel*
Graves	*Château Haut-Brion, Château La Mission Haut-Brion*
Saint Emilion	*Château Ausone, Château Cheval Blanc*
Pomerol	*Château Pétrus*
Sauternes	*Château d'Yquem*

———————— *BURGUNDY* ————————

Chablis	Vaudésir, Les Clos, Grenouilles, Valmur, Blanchots, Preuses, Bougros
Côte de Nuits	Gevrey-Chambertin—*Chambertin, Clos de Bèze, Latricières-Chambertin, Mazis-Chambertin, Chanmes-Chambertin or Mazoyères-Chambertin, Griotte-Chambertin, Ruchottes-Chambertin, Chapelle-Chambertin*
	Morey-Saint-Denis—*Clos de Tart, Clos de la Roche, Clos Saint Denis*
	Chambolle-Musigny—*Musigny, Bonnes Mares*
	Vougeot—*Clos de Vougeot*
	Flagey-Echézeaux—*Grands Echézeaux, Echézeaux*
	Vosne-Romanée—*Romanée-Conti, La Tâche, Romanée-Saint Vivant, Richebourg, La Romanée*
	Nuits-Saint-Georges—*Les Saint Georges*
Côte de Beaune	Aloxe-Corton—*Le Corton, Corton Charlemagne, Corton Clos du Roi, Corton Bressandes*
	Beaune—*Grèves, Fèves*
	Pommard—*Rugiens, Epenots*
	Volnay—*Caillerets, Clos des Ducs, Champans*
	Meursault—*Perrières, Genevrières*
	Puligny-Montrachet—*Montrachet, Chevalier-Montrachet, Bâtard-Montrachet, Bienvenue-Bâtard-Montrachet*
	Chassagne-Montrachet—*Criots-Bâtard-Montrachet*

———————— *RHINELAND* ————————

Mosel-Saar-Ruwer	Piesport—*Goldtröpfchen, Schubertslay*
	Bernkastel—*Doktor, Lay*
	Graach—*Himmelreich, Domprobst*
	Wehlen—*Sonnenuhr, Klosterberg*
	Zeltingen—*Schlossberg, Sonnenuhr*
	Wiltingen—*Scharzhofberg*
Rheingau	Rauenthal—*Baiken, Gehrn*
	Erbach—*Marcobrunn, Steinmorgen*
	Hattenheim—*Steinberg, Nusbrunnen*
	Johannisberg—*Schloss Johannisberg, Hölle*
	Rudesheim—*Berg Rottland, Berg Roseneck*
	also: *Schloss Vollrads, Schloss Eltz, Schloss Reinhartshausen*
Rheinhessen:	Nackenheim—*Rothenberg, Engelsberg*
	Nierstein—*Hipping, Glöck*
	Oppenheim—*Kreuz, Sackträger*
	Bingen—*Scharlachberg, Pfarrgarten*
Rheinpfalz:	Wachenheim—*Gerümpel, Böhlig*
	Forst—*Kirchenstück, Jesuitengarten*
	Deidesheim—*Hohenmorgen, Grainhübel*
	Ruppertsberg—*Gaisböhl, Spiess*

NOTE: There are many other vineyards near each of these that produce outstanding wines (see extended lists in Chapter 3). Many towns and districts tack the names of their best vineyards to their own (as has Gevrey-Chambertin) so some reflected glory will aid the sale of lesser wines.

	millions of gallons produced	gallons consumed per capita
LEADING WINE PRODUCING COUNTRIES AND THEIR ANNUAL CONSUMPTION		
Italy	2,000+	30 – (12 cases, or 144 bottles)
France	2,000+	30 – (2–3 bottles/week)
Spain	1,000+	20 (about 2 bottles/week)
USSR	600–700	4+ (1–2 bottles/month)
Argentina	600–700	20+
United States	400–500	2+ (1 bottle/month)
Portugal	300–400	30+ (3 bottles/week)
Romania	200–250	9 – (1 bottle/week)
West Germany	200–250	6+
Algeria	± 200	minuscule (Moslem)
Yugoslavia	150–200	7+ (3 bottles/month)
Hungary	120–150	10 (4 bottles/month)
Greece	120–150	10
Chile	120–150	10
South Africa	120–150	2+ (1 bottle/month)

Portugal has the largest per capita consumption; the United States is among the smallest consumers of major wine-producing countries.

―――――――――― *BUYING BURGUNDY* ――――――――

The *great* Burgundies, which are among the rarest of wines, come from a single slope called the Côte d'Or (Golden Slope), some thirty miles in length—reds from the northern strip of a dozen miles called the Côte de Nuits, reds and whites from the southern stretch called the Côte de Beaune. A tiny section north of the Golden Slope produces Chablis, but half of the Burgundies we drink come from southern Burgundy, mostly Beaujolais and Mâcon.

Scarcely a third of all Burgundies come from the Golden Slope; many of these are wines bearing the names of the towns whose lines cut across the slope. Vineyards officially rated Great Growths and First Growths (*Grands Crus* and *Premiers Crus*) are so scarce and so in demand that prices start at $10.

There are many good vineyards surrounding the rated growths and there is constant pressure to get them ranked officially. The best of all these wines are considered to be those bottled by the vineyard owners, a practice called estate-bottling; vineyards are divided among several owners, so wines of each vineyard vary. Here is a list of the greatest vineyards along the Golden Slope, for those who want to taste Burgundies of the highest rank.

―――――――――― *Red Côte de Nuits Vineyards* ――――――――

Chambertin and Clos de Bèze	*Noted for its robe, or deep color and clarity, long life, intensity of taste, and remarkable elegance.*
Clos de Tart	*Full and robust, long-lived.*

Clos de la Roche	*Powerful, with great depth of flavor, considered to have somewhat less elegance than the Chambertins.*
Clos Saint-Denis	*Intense and long-lived, concentrated and slow to mature.*
Bonnes Mares	*Powerful and with the breed of a Chambertin, but also possessing some of the finesse of Musigny.*
Musigny	*Noted above all for its finesse, lightness, delicacy.*
Clos de Vougeot	*Noted for breed and bouquet rather than body.*
Grands Echezeaux	*Full, rich.*
Romanée-Conti	*Most famous of Burgundies, distinguished by elegance, balance, rich bouquet.*
Romanée-Saint-Vivant	*Like all Romanées, with a special softness.*
La Romanée	*Vineyard of a scant two acres, now perhaps less distinguished, not quite so elegant and rich as its neighbors.*
La Tâche	*Full and velvety, noted for depth of taste and elegance of bouquet.*
Richebourg	*The fullest and richest of Vosne-Romanées.*

—————— *Red Côte de Beaune Vineyards* ——————

Corton	*Silky rather than velvety; balanced, with great breed.*

NOTE: Vineyards adjoining those of Chambertin and Corton are also ranked as Grand Cru and will say so on the label. Customarily the name of the township does not appear on the label. The vineyard name—and the phrase Grand Cru—is considered enough to identify these magnificent wines. When the name of the township is used, the vineyard name is printed in capitals under the township.

———————— White Côte de Beaune Vineyards ————————

Corton Charlemagne	*Noted for full body and depth of taste.*
Montrachet	*Considered to be the greatest of dry white wines, light greenish-gold in color, noted for its powerful bouquet and breed.*
Chevalier-Montrachet	*With only slightly less depth of flavor than Montrachet, which it adjoins.*
Bâtard-Montrachet	*Like its neighbors and ranked somewhat below them, it often surpasses them.*
Bienvenue-Bâtard-Montrachet	*Perhaps less dry than Bâtard, but certainly its peer.*
Criots-Bâtard-Montrachet	*An extension of Bâtard and indistinguishable from it.*

However tedious the explanation of geography and Grand Cru ratings, to say nothing of the extravagance of listing wines that can cost $20 a bottle and more, nothing less will give a glimmer of what Burgundy can be. The present fashion for drinking white wines has thrown prices out of proportion, the fame of the great Burgundies raising prices of lesser ones far above their worth.

A good southern Burgundy like Pouilly-Fuissé sold for $18 at the beginning of the decade, often $40 in restaurants, while the grander Montrachets and Cortons sometimes sold for less. Even lesser white Mâcons were being sold for $6, many of the good blends from shippers commanding $10. Many shops stopped stocking Burgundies, red or white.

Small crops from the last three vintages of the Seventies have only intensified demand. Even experts grumble, declaring that vines are allowed to bear too many grapes, thus lowering the quality of the wine. There are accusations that the wines are stretched with lesser wines, that the vineyards are extended into soils that produce wines of inferior quality, that wines are hastily vinified to get them on the market quickly. Inflation, the fall of the dollar, and ever-increasing demand have put Burgundy beyond the reach of most of us, directing our attention to wines from other regions of scarcely less distinction. A California Chardonnay at $10 has become a bargain.

By mid-decade, prices may have settled down. Large crops can be expected. For tomorrow, when we can again afford Burgundies, here is a list of the best of them, township by township.

CÔTE DE NUITS

A dozen miles long and sometimes only a couple of hundred yards wide, Côte de Nuits comprises some 3,700 acres of vineyard, the best of them in the curve where the plain meets the height of the southeast-facing slope. The best of the wines bear vineyard names. The wines are expensive; they may take five years or longer to mature and the best of them may continue to develop for a decade. Much of the lesser wine from flatland vineyards is marketed under township names;

blends from several townships are marketed as Côte de Nuits-Villages.

There are more than 400 vineyards known by name along the Côte de Nuits, close to a thousand in the Côte de Beaune. Certainly a couple of hundred deserve to be rated as First Growths, the Premiers Crus, but only those most apt to be exported are listed here. A wine from any of the famous towns of the Golden Slope that bears a vineyard name is almost certainly better than those bearing only town names.

―――――――――――――――― *Fixin* ――――――――――――――――

Splendid, full-bodied wines slow to mature come from this northernmost commune of the Golden Slope. They are still bargains, when they can be found, because they are overshadowed by famous neighbors. Most of the wine from some 300 acres is sold as Côte de Nuits-Villages. About 100 acres of this is sold as Fixin, half of that coming from five vineyards, ranked as Premier Cru, whose wines are considered to be only slightly less grand than the nearby Chambertins. Entire production is only about 10,000 cases in a good year. Leading First Growths are:

     Clos de la Perrière
     Clos du Chapitre
     Les Arvelets
     Les Hervelets
     Clos du Napoléon

―――――――――――――― *Gevrey-Chambertin* ――――――――――――――

Deep in color, full in body, outstanding for that quality variously described as finesse, elegance, and breed. Clos de Bèze, Chambertin, and seven other vineyards that are ranked as Grand Cru, as well as more than a score more that are ranked Premier Cru, occupy a third of the more than 1,000 acres in the commune. Only a few of the first growths are exported; most of the total annual production of some 150,000 cases is sold as Gevrey-Chambertin, good but not great and generally overpriced, thanks to the fame of the Chambertins. Great Growths are listed in capitals, First Growths in upper and lower case.

CHAMBERTIN-CLOS DE BÈZE
CHAMBERTIN
LATRICIÈRES-CHAMBERTIN
MAZIS-CHAMBERTIN
CHARMES- (OR MAZOYÈRES-)
  CHAMBERTIN
CHAPPELLE-CHAMBERTIN
RUCHOTTES-CHAMBERTIN
GRIOTTE-CHAMBERTIN
Clos Saint Jacques
Les Varoilles
Cazetiers
Aux Combottes
Combe aux Moines

Morey-Saint-Denis

Wines only slightly less full and elegant than the Chambertins come from the 250 acres in the township, half of which are rated growths. The wines are overshadowed by the adjoining Chambertins and are bargains when priced below them. Some 25,000 cases are produced in a good year. Great Growths are listed in capitals, First Growths in upper and lower case:

CLOS DE TART
CLOS DE LA ROCHE
CLOS SAINT-DENIS
BONNES MARES
Clos des Lambrays

Les Ruchots
Sorbet or Clos Sorbet
Les Millandes
Clos des Ormes
Monts-Luisants

───────────────── *Chambolle-Musigny* ─────────────────

The elegant red wines noted for light bouquet mark a shift to lightness in wines of the Golden Slope and are traditionally called the most feminine of them. Almost half of some 400 acres of vineyard are rated growths; production is around 60,000 cases a year. Great Growths are listed in capitals, First Growths in upper and lower case:

BONNES MARES
MUSIGNY
Les Amoureuses
Les Charmes
Les Baudes
Combe d'Orveau
Les Cras
Les Sentiers

───────────────── *Clos de Vougeot* ─────────────────

With some 60 owners of the 125 acres of vineyard, there are marked differences in the wine, which is noted for its full bouquet, lingering taste, and such majesty that French troops were supposed to salute as they went by. There are some 20,000 cases of the red wine and a small plot outside the walled vineyard that produces less than 500 cases of white wine, Clos Blanc de Vougeot.

CLOS DE VOUGEOT (Great Growth)
Clos Blanc de Vougeot (First Growth)

--------------------- *Vosne-Romanée* ---------------------

The Romanées are brilliant wines, rich and velvety, with a penetrating bouquet at once fruity and flowery, perhaps the most illustrious of Burgundies. There are nearly 600 acres of vineyard, including the Great Growths of Grands Echézeaux and of Echézeaux, the small township just north, whose lesser wines are marketed as Vosne-Romanée. Rated growths comprise almost half the acreage and the wine sold as Vosne-Romanée is perhaps the best buy of all the wines bearing township names of the Côte de Nuits. Great Growths are listed in capitals, First Growths in upper and lower case.

ROMANÉE-CONTI
LA TÁCHE
ROMANÉE SAINT-VIVANT
RICHEBOURG
LA ROMANÉE
GRANDS ECHÉZEAUX
ECHÉZEAUX
La Grande Rue
Les Malconsorts
Les Suchots
Les Beaux-Monts
Les Petits-Monts
Aux Brulées

--------------------- *Nuits-Saint-Georges* ---------------------

The full, rich wines come from more than 900 acres of vineyard and include those of Prémeaux, which end at a marble quarry that separates the two parts of the Golden Slope. None of the vineyards is ranked as Grand Cru, although some should be; more than a third are rated Premier Cru, and wines sold as Nuits-Saint-Georges are good buys when half the price of the First Growths. Those in the right-

hand column are in Prémeaux, in case you want to compare
the sturdy wines with those of Nuits-Saint-George itself.

Les Saint-Georges	Clos de la Maréchale
Les Cailles	Clos Arlots
Les Vaucrains	Clos des Argillières
Les Pruliers	Clos des Grand Vignes
Les Porrets	Les Perdrix
Les Boudots	Clos des Forêts
Aux Murgers	Les Didiers
Clos de Thorey	Clos des Corvées

CÔTE DE BEAUNE

Soft and charming wines, less commanding than those from
the Côte de Nuits, come from nearly 8,000 acres of vineyard
stretched along fifteen miles of sloping land. Only Corton
among the reds is ranked Grand Cru, but Great Growths
among the whites include the Montrachets and Corton
Charlemagne. Many of the vineyards, particularly of Volnay
and Meursault, but also others, should be rated Great
Growths. They are not as yet, but the best of the First Growths
head the following lists. They are unofficially called *Têtes de
Cuvée*, chief vats, and warrant the higher prices they
command.

Several hamlets and less-well-known townships are
considered in the second rank, perhaps mostly because their
wines are lighter and somewhat less elegant than their
famous neighbors, or because they are ready to drink scarcely
three years after the vintage and may begin to fade after five
years. They are good buys when they can be found and when
they are less expensive than Beaune or Volnay. Much of the
wine is sold as Côte de Beaune-Villages.

Santenay
Monthélie
Auxey Duresses

Saint Romain
Saint Aubin

A charity hospital, the Hospices de Beaune, each November 15 holds an auction of wines from plots that have been donated to it. They are sold under the name of the donor, prices setting the value of the vintage along the Golden Slope. Buying wines at the auction is a mark of prestige; the prices are usually high. Wines to look for from this group are listed below:

> Corton: Charlotte Dumay
> Docteur Peste
> Beaune: Nicolas Rolin
> Guigone de Salins
> Savigny: Arthur Girard
> Forquerand
> Pommard: Dames de la Charité
> Billardet
> Volnay: Blondeau
> Général Muteau
> Meursault: Jehan Humblot

———————————— *Aloxe-Corton* ————————————

The full reds of Corton and big whites of Corton Charlemagne come from some 500 acres of vineyard, Great Growths that produce 30,000 cases of red and 12,000 cases of white wine. Some 50,000 cases of red wine, including that from several vineyards entitled to add Corton to their name, increase the total. Great Growths are listed in capitals, First Growths in upper and lower case:

CORTON
CORTON CHARLEMAGNE
Corton-Clos du Roi
Corton-Bressandes

Corton-Renardes
Corton-Perriers
Corton-Les Maréchaudes
Languettes
Les Pougets

────────────────── *Pernand-Vergelesses* ──────────────────

A hamlet up the slope from Aloxe-Corton has part of Corton in
its 350 vineyard acres, nearly 70 acres of which are Premier
Cru. Total production is about 40,000 cases, usually a good
buy because it is not well known. Leading First Growths are:
Ile des Vergelesses
Les Basses Vergelesses
Creux de la Net
Les Fichots
En Caradeux

────────────── *Beaune and Savigny-les-Beaune* ──────────────

Beaune, the largest township of the Golden Slope with more
than 1,300 acres, and neighboring Savigny with nearly 1,000
acres of lighter wines, are the most easily available of those
from the Golden Slope. More than a quarter million cases are
produced between them, including 10,000 cases of white
wine. The big, rounded wines are good values when priced
well below neighboring Corton and Pommard. Perhaps half
the acreage should be ranked as Premier Cru, the list headed
by Grèves and Fèves.
Grèves
Fèves
Bressandes
Les Cent-Vignes

Champimonts
Clos des Mouches
Clos du Roi
Marconnets
Les Avaux
Les Cras
Aigrots
Clos de la Mousse
Les Theurons
Vergelesses
Lavières
Jarrons
Dominode

──────────────── *Volnay* ────────────────

The most charming of all Burgundies, with great finesse and
an almost silken softness that is usually called velvety, it
outclasses in elegance the more famous neighboring Pommard. Wines labeled simply "Volnay" are often excellent
values, particularly when priced under Pommard or Beaune.
Some 90,000 cases are produced from more than 500 acres.
An additional 10,000 cases, called Volnay Santenots, are
marketed from red wines of neighboring Meursault. Leading
First Growths are:

Caillerets
Clos des Ducs
Champans
Fremiets
Chevret
Clos des Chênes
Les Santenots

--------------------------------- *Pommard* ---------------------------------

The most popular of Burgundies, and consequently over-priced, Pommard has some 800 acres of vineyard producing more than 125,000 cases of soft, fruity, elegant wines. Those with vineyard names far surpass the wide range of bottlings that are called simply "Pommard" on the label. Leading First Growths are:

      Rugiens, Bas or Hauts
      Epenots or Petits Epenots
      Pézerolles
      Clos Blanc
      Chanière
      Charmot
      Chanlins-Bas
      Platière
      Arvelets
      Clos de la Commaraine

--------------------------------- *Meursault* ---------------------------------

Does everyone know that the green-gold wines of Meursault got their name because the white wines are only a mouse-jump away from Volnay's reds? Even those sold as Meursault are big, soft, elegant, rounded wines, surpassed only by those ranked Premier Cru. Meursault is supposed to decline quickly, turning brown (that is, madeirizing or oxidizing) after five years. Bottles kept in a cool and constant cellar, however, are steely and astonishing well into their second decade. Leading First Growths are:

      Perrières or Clos des Perrières
      Genevrières
      Charmes
      Goutte d'Or

--------- *Puligny-Montrachet* ---------

Montrachets are considered the greatest dry white wines on earth, full, balanced, subtle, and grand. Several vineyards are ranked Grand Cru and are permitted to add Montrachet to their names. There are nearly 600 acres of vineyard, those ranked Premier Cru scarcely less glorious. Great Growths are listed in capitals, First Growths in upper and lower case:

> LE MONTRACHET (about half)
> BÂTARD-MONTRACHET (about half)
> CHEVALIER-MONTRACHET
> BIENVENUE-BÂTARD-MONTRACHET
> Chalumeaux
> Les Combettes
> Blagny
> Pucelles
> Clavoillons
> Caillerets
> Folatières

--------- *Chassagne-Montrachet* ---------

The last of the great townships of the Golden Slope shares some of the Montrachet vineyards with neighboring Puligny, but also boasts several vineyards, red and white, that deserve Grand Cru status. They are big, full-bodied wines from nearly 900 acres of vineyard, producing perhaps 120,000 cases in a good year. Great Growths are listed in capitals, First Growths in upper and lower case:

> LE MONTRACHET (about half)
> BÂTARD-MONTRACHET (about half)
> CRIOTS-BÂTARD-MONTRACHET
> Ruchottes
> Caillerets
> Morgeot (also red wines)

---------- *Santenay* ----------

These wines are much less elegant than those of Chassagne, but often extremely good, reds being better than whites. The wines last a long time, sometimes show a not unpleasant earthy taste, called *gôut de terroir*, and can be excellent values when half the price of a Pommard, say. Wines labeled simply "Santenay" are ones to look for; vineyard names rarely indicate significantly better wines. Vineyards from the township to the south—Dezize-les-Maranges, Cheilly-les-Maranges, and Sampigny-les-Maranges—can occasionally be found, but those from the nearly 1,000 acres of Santenay produce well over 120,00 cases and are superior.

---------- *CHABLIS* ----------

A separate district north of the Golden Slope near Auxerre, Chablis is planted entirely in Chardonnay. The least of the wines is marketed as "Petit Chablis," some 50,000 cases meant to be drunk within the year and usually sold in carafe. Wine marketed as "Chablis" is somewhat better and continues good into the second year following the vintage; some 2,000 acres produce 350,000 cases.

Nine vineyards are ranked as Premier Cru. They consist of some 1,000 acres and give fresh dry wines, at their best perhaps three years after the vintage. They have been called flinty, indicating a grand stony quality in the taste, and are the driest of the white Burgundies, classic with oysters, equally superb with ham, trout, and exceptional cold dishes such as aspics and mousses. Some 80,000 cases are produced.

The best of all are the Great Growths, seven Grand Cru vineyards that occupy some 225 acres of a single concave slope shaped much like the shell of one of the oysters they glorify. Only some 35,000 cases are produced in a good year, maximum permitted yield being about 375 gallons per acre.

GRAND CRU	PREMIER CRU*
Vaudésir	Monts de Mileu
Valmur	Montée de Tonnerre
Grenouilles	Fourchaume
Les Clos	Vaucoupin
Les Preuses	Vaillon
Blanchots	Montmains
Bougros	Côte de Lechet
	Beauroy
	Vosgros

There is constant pressure by owners to raise the ratings of their vineyards, but of the 21 once ranked First Growths, several have been grouped as part of the nine listed above, to simplify matters. Stubborn owners cling to the old names, which still may be found on labels, but they will bear the identifying phrase, Premier Cru. Two vineyards ranked below the nine are Les Fourneaux and Melinots. The phrase to look for on the label is Premier Cru; those with no vineyard designation are blends of small lots from several holdings and are excellent, only slightly less wonderful than those called Grand Cru.

---------------------- LESS IS BEST ----------------------

The number of tons of grapes or gallons of wine per acre are limited by law in the best European vineyards. Permitted yields in the best vineyards of Burgundy and Bordeaux are about two tons per acre, about 320 gallons or 125 cases of wine, while First Growths are permitted about 370 gallons (35 hectoliters per hectare).*

A hectare is 2.47 acres; a hectoliter is 26.42 U.S. gallons or 22.03 English imperial gallons. A case of 12 bottles contains about 2.5 gallons of wine.

Following are permitted yields for some Burgundy vineyards.

●*317 gallons/acre or 30 hectos/hectare*●
Chambertin and Chambertin Clos-de-Bèze
Musigny

Bonnes-Mares, Clos Saint Denis, Clos de la Roche, Clos de Tart
Clos de Vougeot
Grands Echézeaux, Echézeaux
Romanée, Romanée Conti, Romanée Saint Vivant, La Tâche, Richebourg
Corton, Corton Charlemagne, Charlemagne
Montrachet, Chevalier Montrachet, Bienvenues-Bâtard-Montrachet, Criots-Bâtard-Montrachet

●*343 gallons/acre or 32 hectos/hectare*●
Charmes-Chambertin, Chapelle-Chambertin, Griotte-Chambertin, Latricières-Chambertin, Mazis-Chambertin, Ruchottes-Chambertin

●*370 gallons/acre or 35 hectos/hectare*●
Chablis Grand Cru, First Growths from the following communes:
Fixin, Gevrey-Chambertin, Morey-Saint-Denis, Chambolle-Musigny, Vougeot, Vosne-Romanée, Nuits-Saint-Georges, Côtes-de-Nuits-Villages
Ladoix-Serrigny, Aloxe-Corton, Pernand-Vergelesses, Savigny-les-Beaune
Chorey-les-Beaune, Beaune, Côte de Beaune, Côte-de-Beaune-Villages
Pommard, Volnay, Volnay-Santenots, Monthélie, Auxey-Duresses, Saint Roman, Meursault, Blagny, Puligny-Montrachet, Chassagne-Montrachet, Saint-Aubin, Santenay, Sampigny- or Cheilly- or Dezize-les-Maranges Mercurey

●*422 gallons/acre or 40 hectos/hectare●*
Chablis Premier Cru:
Givry, Rully, Montagny
Beaujolais:
Brouilly, Côte de Brouilly, Chénas, Chiroubles, Fleurie, Juliénas, Morgon, Moulin-à-Vent, Saint-Amour
●*475 gallons/acre or 45 hectos/hectare●*
Pouilly-Fuissé, Pouilly-Vinzelles, Pouilly-Loché, Saint Véran, Beaujolais-Villages

●*528 gallons/acre or 50 hectos/hectare●*
Mâcon (for reds), Mâcon Supérieur (reds and whites), Mâcon-Villages and Pinot-Chardonnay-Mâcon (for whites)

NOTE: An old wine aphorism has it that the smaller the yield the better the wine.

──────── *BUYING BORDEAUX* ────────

There are a lot of Bordeaux from which to choose—more than 2,000 vineyard names, which are far too many, about 300 of them worth considering. Wines from 175,000 acres produce 90 million gallons in a good year. More than half of it is sold as Bordeaux and Bordeaux Supérieur; another quarter comes from minor districts. All are good, dry ordinary table wines to buy when priced below Côtes-du-Rhône or Rioja or Chianti. But Americans have learned to like the Classed Growths (*Crus Classés*) and those from famous districts with famous names. There are bargains to be found, but only from reading the small print on the labels.

Wines from little-known districts or those ignored can be best buys:

● *Canon Fronsac:* Red wines the Bordelais buy, soft and full-bodied. Somewhat less distinguished are those labeled Côtes-de-Fronsac. Half a million cases.

●*Premières Côtes de Bordeaux:* Pleasing, soft reds; whites less good and often sweet. Half a million cases.

●*Bourg, Bourgeais, Côtes de Bourg:* Often good reds, soft and dry, worth trying when found. Some 1½ million cases.

●*Graves Supérieur:* White wines from dry to dryish, made from Sauvignon Blanc, sometimes blended with Semillon. Among the best buys in low-priced white wines. Some 125,000 cases.

●*Entre-Deux-Mers:* The fashion for white wines has encouraged growers to produce light, dry bottlings sold with the slogan "Entre Deux Huitres," and now one of the pleasantest wines to have with fish as well as oysters. Over 1½ million cases.

Many of these wines cost under $4 as the decade began, many of them in a category that has come to be called *Petits Châteaux.* Even when there is no castle on the grounds, sometimes not even a dwelling at all, vineyards are called *châteaux*, a term that seems to add a certain cachet. The official Appellation Contrôlée ratings appear under the château name on the label.

Wines with district names are good buys, blends from shippers that cost under $5 at at the beginning of the decade. Médoc townships like Margaux, Pauillac, Saint Julien and Saint Estèphe market sound, dry reds; the regional name of Médoc is worth looking for, as are bottles from the townships of Moulis and Listrac. Towns around Saint Emilion are allowed to add that famous name to their own. Also good buys are blends called Saint Emilion, Pomerol, and Graves; these are often passed by because of the mistaken idea that the word *château* on the label indicates a superior wines. Here is a list of these good, dry regional reds, often bargains:

Haut Médoc or Médoc	2 million cases
Moulis or Listrac	300,000 cases
Margaux	400,000 cases
Saint Julien	300,000 cases
Pauillac	300,000 cases

Saint Estèphe	350,000 cases
Pomerol or Lalande de Pomerol	750,000 cases
Saint Emilion	2.5 million cases
Saint Georges-Saint-Emilion	75,000 cases
Montagne-Saint-Emilion	600,000 cases
Puisseguin-Saint-Emilion	200,000 cases

Much of this vast amount of wine is sold under the name of the vineyard—Château whatnot—but those with district or township names are often better buys. Château wines command a premium.*

Buying wines bottled by vineyard owners—Château-bottlings—is bewildering because of the wide price range. Considering price alone on a scale of 100, wines rated Premier Grand Cru Classé are priced at 80 or higher. (These are wines like Château Lafite or Château Haut-Brion, those printed in capitals in the following lists.) Famous wines of the Médoc ranked as Cru Classé over a century ago are priced at 60; Classed Growths not well known are priced at 40, as are those Saint Emilions newly rated as Saint Emilion Grand Cru Classé (some 60 vineyards). And there are the Cru Exceptionel and Cru Bourgeois Growths priced at 20. By this reckoning Château Lafite at $16 would compare in price to a Bourgeois Growth at $4. The Lafite costs four times as much and might be considered only twice as good. The range in price is wider than the range in quality.

There were excellent château-bottlings available in a price range of $5 to $10 as the Eighties began. Although the Bordeaux wines are quite different, you might choose to

---

Rather than offering many wines from unknown châteaux, shippers blend them under brand names. Good buys under $5 include Sichel My Cousin's Claret, de Luze Club Claret, Delor La Cour Pavillon, Dourthe Frères Grande Marque Bordeaux, Mouton Cadet, Dulong Ecu Royal Claret, Calvet Réserve. There are many others worth trying.

compare them with Cabernet Sauvignons of California in the same price range.

Here is a list of Bordeaux châteaux by townships, for comparison:

MÉDOC

The most famous red wines of Bordeaux come from 17,000 acres of gravelly sloping land north of the city of Bordeaux, producing some 4 million cases of wine ranging from exalted splendors that may taste best twenty years after the vintage to a host of splendid wines that are at their best when half that old. The most famous live longest; rated as Premier Grand Cru Classé, they are listed in capitals in the townships from which they come, along with wines that are similar in taste but less grand and much less expensive.

The new wines are stored in new casks so that they will pick up tannin from the new oak. This practice enables them to last a long time, but it is now pretty much limited to the most famous châteaux. Storage in cask once extended for three years, but now wines that mature more quickly are desired and storage in cask is about two years; some lesser wines are matured in vats so that they will be drinkable in three years or less.

Cabernet Sauvignon grapes dominate the vineyard, with some Merlot to hasten the softening of the wine, along with small proportions of Malbec and Petit Verdot.

Margaux

Red wines noted for bouquet and delicacy, these are considered the lightest of Bordeaux and the most elegant. Neighboring townships are marketed as Margaux, greatly increasing the number of elegant wines available. These wines are often tasted against each other to distinguish subtle differences and this is a waste. The wines—splendid with lamb, fowl, roasts of all sorts, cheeses—are meant to be enjoyed, not analyzed. The distinctions are fascinating, however, best appreciated when two or three are served at the same time, in different glasses, with different courses.

When first marketed, three years or so after the vintage, they can cost $8 or more. Leading First Growths are:

CHÂTEAU MARGAUX (Great Growth)
Château Rausan-Ségla
Château Rauzan-Gassies
Château Lascombes
Château Brane-Cantenac
Château Cantenac-Brown
Château Boyd-Cantenac
Château d'Issan
Château Palmer
Château Malescot-Saint-Exupéry
Château Marquis-d'Alesme-Becker
Château Kirwan
Château Giscours
Château Marquis-de-Terme
Château Prieuré-Lichine
Château Pouget

———————————— *Saint Julien* ————————————

Reds considered fuller than those of Margaux, and softer, the first of the Médocs to become ready to drink, often six or eight years after the vintage, although they continue to develop in bottle. They are the first to be tasted when you want to see how a vintage is maturing. They are reasonably priced when first available, at $8 or so. Leading First Growths are:

Château Gruaud-Larose
Château Léoville-Poyferré

Château Léoville-Las-Cases
Château Léoville-Barton
Château Langoa-Barton
Château Beychevelle
Château Talbot
Château Gloria
Château Ducru-Beaucaillou
Château Brainaire-Ducru
Château Lagrange

———————————— *Pauillac* ————————————

The fullest, biggest red wines of the Médoc, Pauillacs are
noted for elegance, consistency, and subtlety. They are the
slowest to develop, often requiring a dozen years and more.
They often cost $10 a bottle, even when bought shortly after
the vintage for future delivery. Great Growths are listed in
capitals, First Growths in upper and lower case.

CHÂTEAU LAFITE-ROTHSCHILD
CHÂTEAU LATOUR
CHÂTEAU MOUTON-ROTHSCHILD
Château Pichon-Longueville-Baron
Château Pichon-Longueville-Lalande
Château Duhart-Milon
Château Clerc-Milon
Château Mouton-Baron-Philippe
Château Pontet-Canet
Château Grand-Puy-Lacoste
Château Grand-Puy Ducasse
Château Lynch-Moussas
Château Lynch-Bages
Château Haut-Bages-Liberal
Château Croizet-Bages
Château Batailley
Château Haut-Batailley
Château Pedesclaux

―――――――――――――――― *Saint Estèphe* ――――――――――――――――

Red wines as full as Pauillacs in many cases, these are less
subtle and very easy to drink. Lesser wines may have an
attractive, earthy taste. Sturdy wines, they are often best
during the second decade after the vintage. When first marketed, they are good buys at $6 or so. Leading First Growths
are:

> Château Beauséjour-Duffau
> Château La Gaffelière
> Château Figeac
> Château Croque-Michotte
> Château Pavie
> Château Ripeau
> Château Trottevielle
> Château l'Angelus
> Château Troplong-Mondot
> Château La Tour-du-Pin-Figeac
> Château Corbin (Gonaud)

―――――――――――――――― *Graves* ――――――――――――――――

Generous red wines noted for elegance and balance, they
develop subtle qualities after ten years. Lesser wines can
become thin and harsh in ordinary years. Less in demand
than the Médocs, they may be more reasonable in price but
can cost $8 or more when a good vintage is marketed. The
white wines are big, soft, yet dry, and elegant. Leading First
Growths are:

> CHÂTEAU HAUT-BRION (Great Growth)
> Château La Mission Haut-Brion
> Château Pape-Clément
> Château La Tour-Haut-Brion
> Château La Tour-Martillac (red and white)
> Château Smith-Haut-Lafite

Château Bouscaut (red and white)
Château Haut-Bailly
Domaine de Chevalier
Château de Fieuzal
Château Carbonnieux (red and white)
Château Malartic-Lagravière
Château Olivier (red and white)

─────────────── *Saint Emilion* ───────────────

From the largest Bordeaux district, almost 20,000 acres, the dry reds are soft and balanced. There are a dozen vineyards rated First Great Growth, more than 60 as Grand Cru Classé. Much Cabernet Franc and Merlot are planted in the vineyards, along with Cabernet Sauvignon. Many of the wines can be drunk five years after the vintage. Many were priced under $6 at the beginning of the decade. Great Growths are listed in capitals, First Growths in upper and lower case:

CHÂTEAU CHEVAL BLANC
CHÂTEAU AUSONE
Château Belair (or Bel-Air)
Château Magdelaine
Château Canon
Clos Fourtet
Château Beauséjour-Becot
Château Beauséjour-Duffau
Château La Gaffelière
Château Figeac
Château Croque-Michotte
Château Pavie
Château Ripeau
Château Trottevielle
Château l'Angelus
Château Troplong-Mondot
Château La-Tour-du-Pin-Figeac
Château Corbin (Gonaud)

---------------------------------- *Pomerol* ----------------------------------

From the smallest of the great districts, even when Lalande-de-Pomerol acreage is included, the wines are the richest of all Bordeaux, thanks to the Merlot grape that predominates in the vineyards. Pomerol has never been officially rated. About a dozen are rated by the trade as second only to Château Pétrus but there are many others. Many of them cost $10 when first on the market, but look for bargains. Leading First Growths are:

      CHÂTEAU PÉTRUS (Great Growth)
      Château Vieux-Château-Certan
      Château Certan
      Château La Conseillante
      Château Beauregard
      Château l'Evangile
      Château La Fleur
      Château La Fleur-Pétrus
      Château Gazin
      Château Latour-Pomerol
      Château Nénin
      Château Petit-Village
      Château La Pointe
      Clos René

---------------------------------- *Crus Exceptionnels du Médoc* ----------------------------------

The vineyards rated Crus Classés in 1855 have been commanding premium prices ever since; all the others have spent the past century and a quarter trying to get their ratings raised. Those rated Exceptional, Supérieur, and Bourgeois growths at various times eventually formed a syndicate. A score of them are now considered to be Exceptional, and two score are considered Great Bourgeois, or Cru Grand Bourgeois (sometimes Grand Cru Bourgeois), and some fifty more are Bourgeois Growths fighting for higher ranking. The French list all these in alphabetical order, but the Exceptional Growths are listed here geographically so that they can be compared with their neighbors.

Château near Margaux:

Angludet*	du Glana
Agassac	Gloria*
Citran	Cantenac
Chasse-Spleen	Ludon
Dutruch-Grand-Poujeaux	Avensan
Poujeaux	Moulis
Fourcas-Dupre	Cussac
Fourcas-Hosten	Saint Julien
Lanessan*	La Fleur Milon Pauillac

Château near Saint Julien:
Caronne-Sainte-Gemme

Château near Saint Estèphe:

Cissac	Haut-Marbuzet
Andron Blanquet	Marbuzet
Beausite	Meyney
Capbern	Phélan-Ségur
Le Crock	

Not ranked, but should be.

——————————— *Crus Grands Bourgeois* ———————————

Bourgeois Growths of the Médoc are exported in some quantity to the United States. While they are considered part of that large class called Petits Châteaux, they should rate higher in the public mind, almost as good as Exceptional Growths and aspiring to the ranks of Classed Growths. The Crus Classés are usually considered more elegant and the wines live longer, perhaps a decade or more. Bourgeois Growths may reach their prime in five years or so. Listed alphabetically, for reference:

Château	*Château*
Beaumont	Le Meynieu
Bel-Orme	Morin
Brillette	Moulin
La Cordonne	Moulin-à-Vent
Colombier Monpelous	Les Ormes de Pex
Coufran	Les Ormes Sorbet
Coutelin-Merville	Patache-d'Aux
Duplessis-Hauchecorne	Paveil de Luze
Fontesteau	Peyrabon
Greyssac	Pontoise Cabarrus
Hanteillan	Potensac
Lafon	Reysson
Lamarque	La Rose Trintaudorn
Lamothe	Segur
Laujac	Sigognac
Liversan	Sociando Mallet
Loudenne	du Taillan
MacCarthy	La Tour de By
Malleret	Tronquoy Lalande
Martinens	Verdignan

――――――――――――― *Crus Bourgeois* ―――――――――――――

Like those ranked Great Bourgeois Growths, those rated Bourgeois Growths do not have any official rating that has been legalized, but represent what the trade thinks of them. These vineyards rank at the top of those now loosely grouped as Petits Châteaux. They are listed alphabetically, for reference:

Château	*Château*
Aney	Haut-Padarnac
Balac	Houbanon
la Bécade	Hourtin-Ducasse
Bellerive	de Labat
Bellerose	Lamothe Bergeron
Bonneau	Landon
le Bosq	Le Landat
le Breuil	Lartigue de Brochon
la Bridane	Lassalle
de By	Lestage
Cap Léon Veyrin	MacCarthy Moula
Carcannieux	Monthil
Castéra	Moulin Rouge
Chambert	Panigon
la Clare	Pibran
la Closerie	Plantey de la Croix
Domaine de la Rose	Pontet
Domaine des Tourelles	Ramage la Batisse
Duplessis-Fabre	la Roque de By
Fonpiqueyre	Saint-Bonnet
Fonréaud	Saransot
Fort Vauban	Soudars
la France	Tayac
Gallais Bellevue	la Tour Blanche
Grand Duroc Milon	la Tour du Mirail
Grand-Moulin	la Tour Haut-Caussan
Haut Bages Moupelou	la Tour Saint-Bonnet
Haut-Canteloup	la Tour Saint-Joseph
Haut-Garin	Vieux Robin

---------------------- *BUYING RHÔNES* ----------------------

Districts scattered along the Rhône produce more than 50 million gallons of wine coming under Appellation Contrôlée laws, more than three-quarters of it Côtes-du-Rhône, the best bargain of all French wines at the beginning of the Eighties. The best wines come from the northern districts below Lyon, from the small districts of Hermitage and Côte Rôtie, and the most famous are in the south, where overpriced Châteauneuf-du-Pape produces a million cases in a good year and where the best of French rosés, Tavel, produces 300,000 cases. But Côtes-du-Rhône is the one to look for. The best of them bear the names of villages:

Gigondas	Cairanne
Cornas	Vacqueyras

Blends of these and others are marketed as Côtes-du-Rhône-Villages. Occasionally, Laudun and Saint Joseph reds can be found, as can Saint Péray whites, all of some interest.

The smallest individual wine granted an appellation is Château Grillet, a full, dry white wine, producing some 600 cases a year. Somewhat more available, and made from the same Viognier grape, is Condrieu, a couple of thousand cases of a superb dry wine drunk locally. It's a mystery why this grape is not planted more widely.

Substantial amounts come from Côte Rôtie, some 16,000 cases of full, velvety red wine that lives for decades. The terraced vineyards are called Côte Brune and Côte Blonde, the latter being naturally considered lighter.

Hermitage and its neighbor Crozes-Hermitage both produce full-bodied wines, red and white. Reds from the Syrah grape are rated among the best in France.

Tavel and neighboring Lirac produce a truly pink wine without orange tones, mostly from the Grenache, a rosé at its best when less than two years old.

All are worth trying when they can be found, especially those labeled simply Côtes-du-Rhône.

──────── *BUYING LOIRE* ────────

There are vineyards all along France's longest river, a multitude of white wines that vary widely, some excellent reds made from the Cabernet Franc of Bordeaux, and a host of rosés, many good. All of the dry wines are best within a couple of years of the vintage.

The reds are from the Middle Loire, fresh, light, and fruity. Look for:

Chinon
Bourgueil
St. Nicolas de Bourgueil
Champigny

Muscadet comes from a large vineyard area, 20,000 acres around Nantes, near the mouth of the Loire. The best is considered to be from Région de Sèvre-et-Main, perhaps fuller and drier than those marketed as Muscadet. To make a bigger wine, grapes are sometimes left with the pulp before pressing. These wines, marketed as Muscadet-sur-lie, are best within three years of the vintage.

─────────── *BUYING WINES OF ALSACE* ───────────

The white wines of Alsace, now high in price, are always marketed with grape names. The best is Riesling, but the most intense in flavor is the Gewürztraminer, which here excels. What is called Tokay d'Alsace is made from Pinot Gris, and is a full-bodied, dry sort of wine with a remarkable richness when five years old. The most plentiful wine is from the Sylvaner, pleasant and soft, but now priced out of the market. Blends are called Zwicker or Edelzwicker, worth trying when under $4 a bottle.

There are some 9 million cases in a good year. The wines are superbly made and good to taste at dinners with wines made from the same grape planted in other regions.

─────────── *BUYING CHAMPAGNE AND OTHER* ───────────
SPARKLING WINES

Champagne, the vineyard region of 50,000 acres sixty miles east of Paris, devised a wine that is the most famous in the world, a cause for celebration and the way to have one. The trick is to catch the bubbles. This is done by adding a little sugar and yeast to the wine, inducing a second fermentation in the bottle. The action captures the resulting bubbles, leaving a sediment that shoots out when the cork is pulled. The bottle is refilled with more wine before the bubbles are lost, then quickly recorked—a tricky business worth the effort because it results in one of the world's great wines.

There are other ways to capture bubbles. The wine can be fermented a second time in a sealed tank, then the bubbles are collected and the two are bottled together. The bubbles are carbon dioxide, a by-product of fermentation. Capturing them separately—called the Charmat Process after its developed—does not produce the fine bubbles that are obtained when the second fermentation takes place in bottle. Charging a wine with carbon dioxide in the way soda water is made is even less preferable, although carbonated wines are made everywhere. So are wines made by the Charmat Process, or bulk process, as well as the Champagne process. However, Champagne, from the Champagne region, is best.

The wines are blended from the juice of Pinot Noir and Pinot Blanc—the juice of both grapes is white—to a style that the firm considers most desirable. Some firms, like Krug and Bollinger and Charles Heidsieck, make full-bodied Champagnes that are in the old tradition. Others, like Taittinger, are lighter in style. Most are in between, like Moët & Chandon or Mumm, two of the most popular. These blends, called *cuvées*, are made so that they will be consistent from year to year; for example, a light vintage is blended with a full one. Vintage Champagnes are made from a single crop that are more expensive but not always appreciably better. Special *cuvées* of exceptional wines are made; they are superb but costly. Part of the price reflects heavy taxes, which amount to a dollar or more a bottle. In the United States the tax applies to all sparkling wines, including bulk process and carbonated, so one might as well buy the best.

Sparkling wines made by the Champagne process are much less expensive because they do not have the cachet of a true Champagne. Many are good buys, particularly those made from white wine in Burgundy (Kriter is the leading brand) and those from the Savoie and from Saint Péray in the Rhône and from Vouvray or Saumur on the Loire. Many of these are bottled to order for an importer or large retailer; to find them, ask the retailer about the house brands.

The second fermentation imparts no sweetness to the wine, which is exceptionally dry, so some sweet syrup is added when the wine is finally bottled. The added sweetness is called the *dosage*. Champagne Nature is driest, with little or no sweetening added. Brut has less than 1.5 percent of sweetness added; this wine is exceptionally dry and the most popular, but is really drier than most people like. Extra Sec has up to 3 percent and is the Champagne that is best with food. Those called Sec or Dry have 4 percent or more, the wine tasting lightly sweet.

There are some 200 brands of Champagne, most of them of exceptional quality, so there are many to like, each slightly different from the others.

Non-vintage Champagnes cost twelve dollars and more at the beginning of the Eighties, vintage Champagnes often cost twenty dollars, special bottlings sometimes twice as much. Many sparkling wines can be found for six or eight dollars, some of the best costing more. The most popular brands include those listed below, but there are many other excellent ones:

Moët et Chandon White Star	Perrier-Jouët Extra Dry
Pommery et Greno Extra Dry	Roederer Brut
Mumm Extra Dry	Bollinger Brut Special Cuvée
Veuve Clicquot White Label	Taittinger Brut La Française
Heidsieck Monopole	Pol Roger Dry Special
Piper Heidsieck Extra Dry	Krug Brut
Charles Heidsieck Extra Dry	
Lanson Black Label	

Sparkling wines from other regions are generally dry and well worth trying when three or four dollars less expensive than Champagne:

Asti Spumante	Piedmont, Italy
Lachrima Christi	Italy
Vouvray or Saumur	Loire, France
Saint Péray	Rhône, France
Seyssel	Savoie, France
Rully	Burgundy, France
Sekt	Germany

Good sparkling wines from California include the following:
> *Brut*
> Korbel
> Hanns Kornell
> Schramsberg
> Almadén
> Domain Chandon
>
> *Extra Dry*
> Hanns Kornell
> Korbel
> Weibel
> Mirassou
>
> *Bulk Process*
> The Christian Brothers
> Weibel
> Almadén
> Inglenook

New York State produces some fine sparkling wines, the best of them being Gold Seal and Great Western.

> *If pleasure you base on drinking the best, damned will you be to drink of the worst.*
>
> Freely, after Montaigne

———————— *SOME SPECIAL FRENCH WINES* ————————

The top 20 percent of all French wines—many of them rarely exported so that we've never heard of most of them—come under Appellation Contrôlée laws. These include wines of the Savoie, like Crépy and Seyssel; of small districts along the Rhône and the Loire; and of the south. Another extensive group, identified by a stamp on the label with the initials VDQS, for *Vins Délimités de Qualité Supérieure*, numbers about 60. Some of these have been elevated to AC status in recent years. They include:

● *Cahors:* A dark, deep wine of the south, made from the Malbec. Once aged in oak for decades and still aged for several years, the wine can take a dozen years or a score to develop. Still low in price at $4 or so, it is a wine to look for.

● *Côtes de Provence:* The rosés of Provence, fresh, fruity, and potent, are the popular summer drink along the Riviera, where it can be bought in demijohns. The best come from Cassis, Bandol, and Bellet. Some of the good ones still carry the VDQS stamp; they are not that much inferior. They should be drunk young, and they should be low in price, under $4.

● *Côtes du Rousillon:* These reds, and whites, from the Pyrenées are interesting enough when low in price, under $4. The best of them are sold as Côte-du-Rousillon-Villages. The practice of adding the word "villages" to wine blended from several towns in a district has become a way to identify superior blends.

At least a few VDQS wines warrant looking for, although they are infrequently imported. They are good buys at less than $4.

● *Cabrieres:* These are pleasant rosés from the Midi, although scarcely in a class with Tavel or Lirac from the Rhône, or Rose de Cabernet of the Loire.

● *Corbières:* Those labeled Supérieur are just that, these big reds of the Midi being the best from that vast area that produces the *vin ordinaire* of France.

●*Minervois:* A full and pleasant Midi red. The Midi districts also produce white and rosé, but they are not interesting to the export market.

●*Côtes du Lubéron:* The rosé is better than the red or white from this district east of Avignon.

NOTE: Wines with grape names and those with brand names may not come under any control laws and may not be worth trying. AC and VDQS identifications on a label are your best guide. An official ranking below VDQS is vin de pays, *label showing its origin. These are rarely exported, nor do they deserve to be.* Vin du pays *are "wines of the countryside," rarely shipped, often not even bottled, meant to be drunk locally, often fair, sometimes delicious. The American practice of making wines as high in alcohol as possible prevents us from having such wines of our own, however local the distribution. There is grumbling about this American style of winemaking, once considered necessary because wines stayed so long on shop shelves. Wines move quickly through distribution channels today, often in a few weeks, so long shelf life is no longer a need. The Eighties should produce many light American wines, as fresh and appetizing—and to be drunk as casually—as the country wines of Europe. There they are disappearing, here they will be coming into their own. A few are already being made, for instance the Riesling of San Martin; they are called "soft" wines, often too light in acids, but growing popularity may induce changes. Of all American wines, these are the most needed to round out the range of what is available. They should be tasted whenever they appear on the market.*

———————— *BUYING RHINES AND MOSELLES* ————————

The fashion for drinking dry white wines apart from meals has encouraged the Germans to devise a new category for their wines, *trocken*, which means dry. Rules state that they can't make the word prominent on a label, so they put on a garland of vines: yellow for dry, green for half-dry, and brown for sweet wines. The garland can't be prominent, either, because there are already two categories for dry wines regularly exported QbA and Kabinett. These are prominent and should be looked for.*

Germans have always drunk their wines apart from meals, progressing along the range of sweetness from Spätlese (flowery and sometimes fruity wine made from grapes picked late), to Auslese (from selected over-ripe bunches that make fruity wine tending to sweetness), then to Beerenauslese (sweet wine from selected berries), and Trockenbeerenauslese (richly sweet wine from selected dried berries). Those who insist they like only dry wines, need to know the grades to avoid more sugary wines.

Kabinett and QbA are delicious with meals, especially with fish and seafood, anything smoked, and spicy dishes. They are good with Oriental dishes, creamy dishes, all kinds of sausages.

Kabinett wines are light in alcohol, about 11 percent, and are made only with natural sugar from the grape. QbA wines are regional blends, with sugar added to the fermentation so that the resulting wine will approach 11 percent. Only in good years can much sweet wine be made, and the excellence of a vintage is often expressed in percentages of

---

*QbA, *for Qualitätswein bestimmter Anbaugebiete,* is worthy of regional designation and worth exporting. Kabinett is the first grade of special category wines (*Qualitätswein mit Prädikat*) and is worth looking for. Tafelwein is ordinary, not deserving of export.

QbA, Kabinett, and sweet wines produced. The small crop of 1978 was nearly 70 percent QbA; scarcely 25 percent was of superior grades, most of that Kabinett. Although not considered to be much of a vintage, according to the charts, Kabinett wines are very good, light and fresh for drinking in the early Eighties.

Names for places German wines come from were sorted during the Seventies to match those of other countries in the Common Market. Eleven regions were designated, as were districts (called *Bereichen*), and areas within them of similar terrain (called *Grosslagen*, or big vineyards). A Grosslage take the name of an important vineyard and may include wines from several townships.

The purpose of the new regulations was to reduce the overwhelming number of vineyard names from 25,000 to a mere 2,500. Vineyards of less than a dozen acres were combined into Grosslagen. (Germans pluralize by adding *n*; they localize by adding *er*, the way a New York resident is a New Yorker.)

Wines are simple; naming them is not. Famous vineyards that were large enough retained their names, identified on the label by *Einzellage*, an individual site. The most specific names are supposed to identify the most distinctive wines, and do, but a Grosslage is a single slope, a Bereich is a blend from similar slopes, their wines not to be ignored. The following lists of wines are from the regions most exported, by district and township—or Bereich and Grosslage, as the Germans say.

─────────────── *Mosel, Saar, Ruwer* ───────────────

The lightest of German wines, these are fresh and delicate, the best of them coming from the Mittel Mosel, some fifteen miles of steep slate vineyards above the coiling river, downstream from Trier. Saar and Ruwer tributaries upstream provide steely, greenish tart wines from rolling vineyards; they are the most glorious, lightest wines in the world, but only in the best of years. The Germans call them sunfire, stargold, cool moonlight—Sonnenfeuer, Sternengold, Kuhlen Mondlicht-stein. In a good year, all of the Mosel provides 30 million gallons from close to 30,000 acres, the best of them listed below. Quality grades of QbA and Kabinett may cost under $5 and are simply not to be missed.

In many townships there are several individual sites. Some of the most prominent listed below:

Townships*	Grosslagen (general site)	Einzellagen (individual site)
Mosel		
Piesporter	Michelsberg	Falkenberg, Goldtröpfchen
Brauneberger	Kurfürstlay	Juffer
Bernkasteler	Kurfürstlay or Badstube	Doktor, Graben, Lay
Graacher	Münzlay	Himmelreich
Wehlener	Münzlay	Sonnenuhr
Zeltinger	Münzlay	Schlossberg
Erdener	Schwarzlay	Busslay
Urziger	Schwarzlay	Würzgarten

Gemeinde or *Ortsteil* is a township or vineyard area within a district, like Volnay in Burgundy or Margaux in Bordeaux, a place name often appearing with the vineyard name on a label.

Saar

Wiltingener	*Scharzberg*	*Braune Kupp*
Kanzemer	*Scharzberg*	*Altenberg*
Oberemmeler	*Scharzberg*	*Hütte*
Ockfener	*Scharzberg*	*Bockstein*

NOTE: Scharzhofberg is a vineyard so reknowned that it does not bear the name of a town on the label, only its own.

Ruwer

Eitelsbacher (or Trierer)	*Römerlay*	*Karthauser Hofberg*
Kaseler	*Römerlay*	*Nieschen*

NOTE: Maximin Grunhaus is a large vineyard, labels usually carrying the name of sections: Herrenberg, Bruderberg, etc.

Rheingau

The noblest of Rhines—full, balanced, with great distinction—lie above a western swerve of the river along a twenty-mile stretch between Rudesheim and Wiesbaden, some 7,500 acres of vineyard that extend south to Hochheim, the name from which the English coined *hock*, their word for all German wines. All but a quarter of the vines are Riesling, the region producing about 6 million gallons in a good year. Some of the vineyards are so famous—Schloss Johannisberger, Schloss Vollrads, Steinberger—that their names alone appear on the label.

The lightest wines are drunk within a year or two of the vintage, as with other German wines, but in great years the Kabinetts and the grades of sweet wines may take four years or longer to reveal themsclves. QbA here deserves being named Qualitätswein, for they are fruity and have big bouquets. Many of the wines, nearly 200, are marketed under vineyard names, more distinctive than those district or general vineyard names.

In many townships there are several individual sites. Some of the most prominent are listed below:

Township	Grosslagen	Einzellagen
Rudesheimer	Burgweg	Berg Roseneck
Geisenheimer	Burgweg	Kläuserweg
Johannisberger	Erntebringer	Hölle
Winkeler	Honigberg	Hasensprung
Hallgartener	Mehrhölzchen	Schönhell
Hattenheimer	Duetelsberg	Hassel
Erbacher	Mehrhölzchen	Marcobrunn
Kiedricher	Heiligenstock	Sandgrub
Eltviller	Steinmächer	Sonnenberg
Rauenthaler	Steinmächer	Baiken, Gehrn
Hochheimer	Daubhaus	Domdechany

——————————— *Rheinhessen* ———————————

A region of soft, full wines, running west to Bingen and south to Worms, this is the original home of Liebfraumilch. Some 55,000 acres produce 50 million gallons, more than a third from Müller-Thurgau, more than a quarter from Silvaner (so spelled in Germany); but the best wines come from a scant 5 percent planted in Riesling. All should be sought after, of course, because the mild, attractive wines are offered at less than $4, though the Rieslings run higher. Müller-Thurgau is named after the man who crossed Silvaner with Riesling, which ripens early and produces a lot of wine soon ready to drink. Of the many townships, the following quartet produce some of the best wines available. Vineyard names are important when you want the best wines.

NOTE: *There are a couple of dozen Grosslagen and nearly 500 vineyard names from more than a gross of villages, most of which end in* heim. *Wines of Grosslagen are good buys when priced with Liebfraumilch or lower.*

In many townships there are several individual sites. Some of the most prominent are listed below.

Townships	Grosslagen	Einzellagen
Niersteiner	Spiegelberg, Auflangen, Rehbach, Gutes Domtal	Hipping, Glöck, Orbel, Krantzberg
Nackenheimer	Spiegelberg, Auflangen	Rothenberg, Engelsberg
Oppenheimer	Güldenmorgen, Krötenbrunnen	Sackträger
Bingen (includes Budesheim, Kempten)	Sankt Rochuskapelle	Scharlachberg

——————————— *Nahe* ———————————

Lively, fruity, fresh wines come from the 10,000 acres of vineyard planted along the river that runs into the Rhine near Bingen. Scarcely known outside the Rhineland, they are among the best buys when they can be found. Planted about equally in Riesling, Müller-Thurgau, and Silvaner, there are many experimental vines to sharpen the 10 million gallons produced each year.

In many townships there are several individual sites. Some of the more prominent are listed below:

Townships	Grosslagen	Einzellagen
Schloss Böckelheim	Rosengarten, Burgweg	Berg, Oberberg
Kreuznacher	Kronenberg	Rosenberg

Rheinpfalz

Full-bodied, with big bouquets, the best of the wines come from the Mittel Hardt and a quartet of townships, listed below. There are more than 50,000 acres of vineyard with Müller-Thurgau and Silvaner predominating, but more than 6,000 acres of Riesling make the best wines. There are many experimental vines, notably 2,000 acres of a Riesling cross called Kerner, which you should look for. The German Weinstrasse begins near the French border and runs along the foothills of the Haardt mountains through wine village after village. Mountains protect what was called the wine cellar of the Holy Roman Empire, fig trees and palms and almonds growing at a latitude the same as Winnepeg's. The lesser wines have an earth taste, called *Bodengeschmack*, not always unpleasant. Auslesen grades from the Riesling are highly prized and among the most expensive.

In many townships there are several individual sites. Some of the more prominent are listed below:

Townships	Grosslagen	Einzellagen
Wachenheimer	*Mariengarten*	*Gerümpel*
Forster	*Mariengarten, Schnepfenflug*	*Jesuitengarten*
Deidesheimer	*Mariengarten, Hofstück*	*Hohenmorgen*
Ruppertsberger	*Hofstück*	*Hoheburg*

Franken and Neighbors

Franconia, the land along the Main, with major vineyards around Würzburg, is the home of Steinwein, bottled in a squat, round flask called *Bocksbeutel*. This bottle is still in use, but the wines are now called Frankenwein, fruity, soft, and good values when under $4. Running south along the east banks of the Rhine, opposite Alsace and extending to the Swiss border, are Hessische Bergstrasse and Baden. Wines from this area are now being imported; they are fruity and fragrant, sometimes soft, sometimes sharp, and best when young.

The Rhineland and its tributaries provide an ocean of white wines, more and more popular as the demand for French wines lifts prices. Most Rhines can be sold in the United States for three or four dollars; fruity and often lightly sweet, they have wide appeal. Much wine comes from modern cooperatives, to be sought after and tasted with other wines that cost about the same.

Rieslings That Aren't

Riesling is the grape planted in all the best Rhineland vineyards. It is called White Riesling on Johannisberg Riesling in the United States. There is a lesser, similar grape called Welschriesling on the Rhine and the Italian Riesling in eastern Europe. Other names for this grape are:

Italy	Riesling italico
Hungary	Olasz Rielsing
Romania	Riesling de Italie
Bulgaria	Italiansky Rizling
Yugoslavia	Taljanska grasevina
Czechoslovakia	Riesling talianski
Russia	Risling italianski

In California, what is marketed as Riesling is wine of the Sylvaner grape, which is called Frankenriesling in Germany, Johannisberg in Switzerland. The Grey Riesling is also the Rülander and Chauché Gris. In California, Emerald Riesling is a cross producing ordinary wine. There is, however, only one true Riesling.

BUYING ITALIAN WINES

Italian wines will be bargains through the first years of the Eighties. French prices have soared: demand for their famous wines is worldwide, and the weak dollar does not make sales here attractive for the French. The Italians, once content to sell a few famous names, are now entering the market with their best wines and are holding down their prices. As the decade began, half of all imported wine was Italian.

But one must still shop around, and taste. Recent increased sales have been mostly in sweetish Lambrusco and bland jug wines, their popularity influencing the way wines are made for the American market. The big shippers make soft wines without any sharpness, big wines high in alcohol, about 13 percent. Most people like them because the prices are right. But limited bottlings have begun to appear.

Acute buyers have begun scouring the wine country for small producers who make distinctive wines, perhaps only a few hundred cases or a few thousand, not enough for national distribution but enough for discerning shopkeepers in major markets. Those not hesitant about trying wines with strange names and unfamiliar labels will make discoveries.

Italy means "land of wine," a corruption of *oenotria tellus*. Buying wine in Italy is easy because there are vineyards everywhere, and news of the wines has always been by word of mouth. Romans rush into the countryside and buy gallons whenever they hear of a particularly good lot—the original grapevine, rumor by gossip. Wines are known by the regions they come from, with scant concern for particular vineyard or vintage, tradition being to drink local wines.

The number of places recognized under recent control laws is approaching 200; a scant dozen were exported a generation ago, most of it Chianti; there are perhaps two score being brought in today and much of it is still Chianti. Lambrusco—red, sweetish, and slightly fizzy—is the largest import. Soft jug wines account for much of the rest, but the best wines from Alpine foothills are widely distributed and these are bargains at $4 and $5.

DOC, for *Denominazione di Origine Controllata*, is the monogram to look for on neck labels, with DOCG (the above, plus *e Garantita*) identifying a few of the best, produced under more strict quality regulations. The brief list below includes the best wines imported from the 2 billion gallons made each year. Wines from each province are listed roughly in order of excellence.

Piedmont	*Lombardy*	*Veneto*
Gattinara	*Valtellina:*	*Valpolicella*
Barolo	*Inferno*	*Bardolino*
Barbaresco	*Sassella*	
Freisa	*Grumello*	
Asti Spumante	*Spanna*	

NOTE: The best reds of the Piedmont and Lombardy are made from the Nebbiolo grape, also called Spanna; other grapes include Freisa, Barbera, and Grignolino, so identified on labels. Superiore *identifies wines aged a year in cask,* riserva *identifies wines held three or four years,* recioto *employs some raisinized grapes, the wines usually sweet, although Recioto della Valpolicella designated* Amarone *is dry. Asti Spumante, once a sweetish sparkling wine, is now made dry and considered to be Italy's best.*

Tuscany	*Trentino-Alto Adige*	*White Wines*
Chianti	*Santa Maddalena*	*Soave*
Chianti Classico	*Lago di Caldaro*	*Cortese*
Chianti Rufina		*Verdiso*
Vino Nobile di		*Verdicchio*
Montepulciano		*Frascati*
Brunello di		*Orvieto*
Montalcino		

NOTE: Young Chianti in straw-colored bottles called fiaschi *can be delicious when a year or two old. Chiantis in regular bottles are best after four years. The dry whites are best drunk young, within a year or two.*

———————— *BUYING JEREZ, XERES, SHERRY* ————————

The delights of sherry missed a generation or two, scorned as a tipple for sly old ladies or as the drink that was proffered when conversation lagged in the drawing room. Like Port and Madeira, the others in the trio of fortified wines that experts consider great, Sherry was relegated to the kitchen. Besides, it was sweet, and anybody in the know wants drinks as dry as they can be. Now people have begun tasting Sherries again, finding among them the world's driest wine, discovering that it is, along with Champagne, the best of all wines to drink during the day.

Wines of the south change wildly because they lack stabilizing fruit acids, but they could be held to a taste by adding brandy and by blending. No wine benefits so much by exploiting these secrets. The pressed juice is fermented in small casks, then separated into types. Exceptionally fragrant—*oloroso* in Spanish—casks are set aside to become Cream and Brown Sherries when old sweetening wines are added to them. Wines that smell and taste nutty are aged to become Amontillados, which means they are like the wines of Montilla. Wines in some casks develop a film of yeast called the *flor*, and this flower gives a dry wine with the smell of freshly baked bread. The wines are called *Finos*, for fine.

The various wines go into separate *criaderas* or cradles, tiers of casks holding older wines of the same type. There are usually three tiers, wine being drawn off from the one containing the oldest wine, which is refilled from the next oldest, which is refilled with the most recent vintage. Wine may take three or more years to get out of the cradle.

The wines then pass through another system of tiered barrels called the *solera*, or foundation. There are never fewer than three tiers in a *solera*, often more, and no more than half the wine in the oldest tier is drawn off in any one year; usually it is much less. Wines from various *soleras* of the same type are blended to make the style for which the house has become famous. Some *soleras* are a century or more old and Jerezanos like to say that some of the oldest wine is in any that is drawn off. Young wines take on the character of the older wines as they pass through the various tiers.

This complication takes place in Jerez, a small town south of Sevilla. There, cathedral-like storehouses display long rows of casks stacked three or four high in moted twilight, silent, echoing with the talk of workers trundling barrels, drawing off wines, filling casks. There is nothing solemn there; the silence is noisy with expectation.

Finos are the dry wines. An Irishman named Garvey arrived in Jerez last century and was disappointed to find that most Sherries were sweet, tasting brown and old. They were wonderful enough but he felt something else could be done. He blended the young Finos, naming the result after Ireland's Patron Saint. Now that is the Sherry most drunk in Spain. It is served cool, even icy, with saucers of almonds or shrimp, peanuts or mountain ham, olives or local cheese. The Spanish can spend a morning with a glass or so, or an afternoon—and dinner is late in Spain, after eleven o'clock, so there is time for Finos as darkness comes. There must be a hundred Finos, but try the one Garvey made, Fino San Patricio. Or try Tio Pepe from Gonzales-Byass, or La Ina from Pedro Domecq.

Finos that are matured on the coast, in Sanlucar de Barrameda, pick up a tang—from the sea air, it is claimed—almost of salt, with a paralyzing dryness that must be tasted. There is no better wine for cold fish or seafood with mayonnaise, unless it is a Fino of Jerez. Those from Sanlucar have a name of their own, Manzanilla, a fresh and yeasty revelation.

Finos should not only be drunk cool. They should be drunk fresh. A newly opened bottle loses its miraculous taste after a day or two, some say even after a few hours. The wine continues to be good—Sherries never seem to die—but it is nothing like the taste of Fino from a newly opened bottle.

The Finos will be less hard to find during the

Eighties—major wine shops always stock a few for lovers of the wines—but Manzanillas are rare; look for La Gitana or La Guita, or any others you can find.

Amontillados are generally available; seek out little-known brands, for excellence is general, as it is in Port or Champagne.

Spanish Sherry is copied everywhere, but none can compare with the wines from Jerez.

——————— BUYING CALIFORNIA WINES ———————

There are those who believe California is the world's new great wine region, ranking with Bordeaux, Burgundy, and the Rhineland. Californians know it's so. Wines of the last decade have shown they may be right; wines of the Eighties may be proof. Only taste will tell.

The wines of California have their own style, developed out of necessity and based on European tradition, scientific experiment, and the good old American desire to succeed. The California style is so pronounced that it is changing wines everywhere.

Necessity stems from limitations of climate, for California has a Mediterranean climate, with cool spots. Parts of the coastal regions are like the best of Europe, although the growing seasons do not stress the vines so much, and that stress is considered necessary to the making of great wine. Grapes have a tendency to lack acid and there is difficulty in obtaining a perfect balance with sugar in the grapes; this problem is pretty well overcome by skill in tending vines and controlling fermentations. Rarely being able to emphasize the dryness of Bordeaux or Burgundy, wines of California emphasize fruitiness and softness.

European tradition emphasized full-bodied wines for export, high in alcohol, because alcohol helps keep a wine from falling apart when shipped and holds it together long enough for it to develop subtlety. Since Americans in general became used to wines high in alcohol—12 percent or more—these are the wines that are made. The wines are often less subtle than European counterparts, however; nor do they seem to live so long. The fact that they develop faster is not considered much of a drawback in California—the claim that one must wait and see is voiced everywhere—and some feel that the wines are quite subtle enough. Still, Californians seek ever more complexity, a quality discussed constantly among the wine growers.

Research has developed new strains of noble varieties, supervines, new ways of handling them in the vineyards, and new ways of handling grapes in the fermenting vats. Long, cool fermentations of white wines prevent unwanted secondary qualities from developing, but the complaint is heard that many fermentations are too long and too cool, producing strong wines that are overdeveloped in certain ways. Some say they are like weight lifters or wrestlers, wines that exaggerate basic characteristics—Chardonnay is too Chardonnay, Cabernet is too Cabernet. California style is too much of a good thing—too fruity, too alcoholic, or too forthright. More is not always better.

Breed, elegance, finesse, and subtlety are lacking in California wines, it is said. This criticism rankles Californians, who struggle to prove the critics wrong. We are not trying to make Bordeaux or Burgundy, they insist, but wines from the great grapes that are typical of California. So they say, but there are constant tastings of Californian against wines of the greatest European vineyards—and exultation about qualities that match or excel foreign bottlings along with minimizing of shortcomings. Just as Burgundians belittle Bordeaux, and vice versa, Californians find shortcomings in European wines. This is good for Europeans, who find they can't pawn off poorly made famous wines as superior; and it is equally good for Americans, who are encouraged to do better and better, discovering that they can.

There is another factor that divides California wine-makers from their European peers. Burgundians have worked with their few noble vines for centuries, the Bordeaux wine-makers have done the same with theirs, and so have Rhine-landers. Details of the techniques have been perfected, even raised to the level of art. A Californian is not so limited, nor so sophisticated. He uses the vines from all these regions, planted side by side. He must become expert in handling Pinot and Cabernet and Riesling, perhaps also the Gamays, Zinfandel, Petite Sirah, and several more varieties. Each of these varieties requires special handling—how long to leave the grapes on the vine, how to ferment, whether to age in wood for a few weeks or a few months—a confusion of detail that can be overwhelming. The vintage in Burgundy is done at one time, those of Bordeaux and the Rhine at others. The Californian has to pick in succession as the grapes are ready, Riesling one day, Cabernet another. Sometimes the variations are just too much to handle properly, or there isn't enough time.

Experiment is constant in all such details. The result is that California wines vary enormously—on a high level in most cases—as to fruitiness, body, and all the things that make one wine different from another. Some Zinfandels are light, some are full, some are dry, some are fruity, some are picked late and some early, some are aged long in oak and some are aged for short periods. This variance can be delight-ful, but the wines are hard to characterize. The essence of the California style is a confusion of excellences as well as an exaggeration of basic characteristics of each variety.

As in any other wine country, any consideration of California wines centers on the best of them, what were called premium wines. This was to distinguish them from the standard wines—those made by the bulk producers—which were given generic names—chablis, burgundy, chianti, rhine and so on—blends of no distinction.

Premium wine producers took to calling their bottlings after the variety of grape from which they were made. Called varietals, these wines once had to contain 51 percent of the grape for which it was named. The percentage was recently raised to 75, a proportion common in many vineyard regions. Recently, however, bulk producers also have taken to marketing wines with grape names, and some of them are remarkable. They are inexpensive, well made, and as good as regional wines made anywhere. They are different, though, fruity and less dry, sometimes even blander than European imports.

The largest of the premium producers market wines that are higher in price than those of bulk producers, and often higher in quality as well. Three of them—The Christian Brothers, Paul Masson, and Almadén—dominated the premium wine market. A few others—Charles Krug, Cresta Blanca (part of Guild), Inglenook (part of Heublein)—took part of the market. The surge of interest during the Seventies led to expansion by others, such as Louis Martini, Wente Bros., Sebastiani, Mirassou, Beaulieu Vineyards. Some bulk producers switched to premiums—Perelli-Minetti, Papagni— and some large new vineyards and estates were formed: The Monterey Vineyard, Robert Mondavi, Sonoma Vineyards, San Martin, Weibel. The list is long, and the wines of all of them are worth seeking. They are among the best on the market at their price levels.

Everybody was producing premium wines, it seemed, so the phrase lost meaning. Call them by their grape names, varietals, and let it go at that.

Great attention was focused on smaller wineries, boutiques they came to be called, first in the Napa Valley, then in Sonoma and Mendocino and Lake, all counties north of San Francisco Bay. There were more of them south of the Bay, mostly in Santa Clara and San Luis Obispo. The area still farther south began opening up in Monterey and Santa

Barbara; in this area, called the Central Coast, more boutique wineries opened, some of them not small at all.

There are a couple of hundred small wineries to choose from and thousands of wines. A selection of some that produce about 25,000 cases or less appears listed by region on page 94.

The largest California wineries, those that produce more than 100,000 cases a year, market many varietals (see below). Some of them, the unfamiliar names, sell wines in bulk, marketing no national brands. Note that Gallo, the country's largest winery, is larger than the next four together.

──────── *CALIFORNIA'S LARGEST WINERIES* ────────

Winery	Storage Capacity (millions of gallons rounded off)	Winery	Storage Capacity (millions of gallons rounded off)
E & J Gallo	226	Delicato Vineyards	8
United Vintners	95	Bronco Winery	6
Guild Wineries	57	East-Side Winery	6
Vie Del	36	Woodbridge Vineyard	5
Bear Mt. Winery	32	Delano Growers	5
Franzia Brothers	28	Bisceglia Bros.	4
Paul Masson	28	Lodi Vintners	4
The Christian Brothers	28	Charles Krug	4
Almadén Vineyards	28	Papagni Vineyards	4
Sierra Wine Corp.	26	Sonoma Vineyards	4
Perelli-Minetti	20	Cucamonga Vineyards	3
California Growers	16	Sebastiani Vineyards	3
Giumarra Vineyards	11	Del Rey Coop.	3
California Mission	9	Liberty Winery	3
Gibson Wine	9	Louis Martini	3
Brookside Vineyards	8	Beringer Vineyards	2

Mirassou Vineyards	2	Buena Vista	*1*
Wente Bros.	2	J. Filippi Vintage Co.	*1*
Frei Bros	2	Novitiate Wines	*1*
Geyser Peak Winery	2	San Antonio Winery	*1*
The Monterey Vineyard	2	Cambiaso Winery	*1*
Napa Valley Coop.	2	Simi Winery	less
Rio Vista Winery	2		than 1
San Martin Vineyards	2	J. Pedroncelli Winery	less
Selma Winery	2		than 1
Robert Mondavi Winery	2	Guglielmo Winery	less
Barengo Vineyards	2		than 1
Seghesio Winery	2	Rutherford Hill Winery	less
Weibel, Inc.	2		than 1
California Products	1	Concannon Vineyards	less
Noble Vineyards	1		than 1
Villa Armando	1	Soda Rock Winery	less
Beaulieu Vineyards	1		than 1
Parducci Winery	1	Sterling Vineyards	less
Foppiano Wine	1		than 1
Korbel & Bros.	1		

NOTE: *Wineries that make mostly varietal wines appear in the regional listings that follow.*

FAMOUS CALIFORNIA WINERIES
IN GENERAL DISTRIBUTION

Napa Wineries

Beaulieu Vineyards (BV)
Beringer Winery
Burgess Cellars
Chappellet Vineyards
Chateau Montelena
Christian Brothers Winery
Clos du Val
Conn Creek Winery

Cuvaison Cellars
Domaine Chandon
Franciscan Vineyards
Freemark Abbey Winery
Heitz Wine Cellars
Inglenook Vineyards
Hanns Kornell Cellars
Charles Krug Winery

Louis Martini Winery
Robert Mondavi Winery
Joseph Phelps Vineyards
Rutherford Hill
Schramsberg Vineyards
Spring Mountain Vineyards
Stag's Leap Wine Cellars
Sterling Vineyards
Sutter Home Winery

Sonoma Wineries

Buena Vista
Chateau St. Jean
Davis Bynum Winery
Dry Creek Vineyard
Geyser Peak Winery
Grand Cru Vineyards
Italian Swiss Colony
Kenwood Vineyards
Korbel & Bros
Pedroncelli Winery
Sebastiani Vineyards

Simi Winery
Sonoma Vineyards
Souverain Cellars
Trentadue Winery

Mendocino Wineries

Cresta Blanca
Fetzer Vineyards
Parducci Wine Cellars
Weibel Wine Cellars

Santa Clara

Almadén Vineyards
Paul Masson Vineyards
Mount Eden Vineyards
Novitiate of Los Gatos
Pedrizzetti Winery
Ridge Vineyards
San Martin Vineyards
Turgeon & Lohr

The Hidden Wines of California

Small wineries producing a few thousand cases a year, perhaps only a few hundred, are rather cutely called boutique wineries. Some sell in major markets, some only at the vineyard or by mail. Some large wineries, and some of the newer ones, sell only in California. Prices can be high, as much as $20 a bottle for a Cabernet or Chardonnay. Some are reasonable, and the wines are always worth trying when you can find them. There are glorious bottles hidden in the cellars.

Napa

Alatera Vineyards
Beckett Cellars
Buehler Vineyards
Cakebread Cellars
Carneros Creek Winery
Cassayre-Forni Cellars
Caymus Vineyards
Chateau Chevalier
Diamond Creek Vineyards
Green & Red Vineyards
Grgich-Hills Cellars
Hill Winery
Keenan Winery
Long Vineyards
Markham Winery
Mayacamas Vineyards
Mount Veeder Winery
Napa Vintners
Napa Wine Company
Nichelini Vineyards
Niebaum-Coppola
Pecota Winery
Pope Valley Winery
Raymond Vineyard
Ritchie Creek Vineyard
Saint Clement Vineyard
Saint Helena Wine
   Company
Sattui Winery
Silver Oak Cellars
Smith Madrone Vineyards.
Stag's Leap Winery
Stonegate Winery
Stony Hill Vineyard

Trefethen Vineyards
Tulecay Winery
Veedercrest Vineyards
Villa Mount Eden
Vose Vineyards
Yverdon Vineyards
Z-D Wines

Sonoma

Alexander Valley Vineyards
Bandiera Wines
Cambiaso Winery
Dehlinger Vineyard
Field Stone Winery
Foppiano Wine Company
Gundlach-Bunschu Wine
   Company
Hacienda Wine Cellars
Hanzell Vineyard
Hop Kiln Winery
Jade Mountain Winery
Johnson's of Alexander
   Valley
Jordan Vineyard
Lambert Bridge
Landmark Vineyards
Lytton Springs Winery
Mark West Vineyards
Martini & Prati Wines
Matanzas Creek
Giuseppe Mazzoni
Mill Creek Winery
Pastori Winery
Preston Winery
Rafanelli Winery

Rege Wine Company
Sausal Winery
Seghesio Winery
Shilo Vineyards
Sotoyome Winery
Stemmler Winery
Swan Vineyards
Valley of the Moon Winery
Vina Vista Vineyards

Mendocino

Edmeades Vineyards
Husch Vineyards
Milano Winery
Navarro Vineyards

Alameda

Richard Crey Winery
Montclair Winery
Morris Port Works
Oak Barrel Winery
Rosenblum Cellars
Stony Ridge Winery
Wine and the People

Lake

Lake County Vintners
Lower Lake Winery

Santa Clara

Bertero Winery
Congress Springs Vineyards
Conrotto Winery
Fortino Winery
Gemello Winery

Giurlani & Bro. Guglielmo
   Winery
Hecker Pass Winery
Kirigin Cellars
Kruse Winery
La Purisma Winery
Ronald Lamb Winery
Live Oaks Winery
Page Mill Winery
Martin Ray Vineyards
Richert & Sons Winery
Sommelier Winery
Sycamore Creek Vineyards

Santa Cruz

Ahlgran Vineyard
Bargetto's Sant Cruz Winery
David Bruce Winery
Devlin Wine Cellars
Felton-Empire Vineyards
Parsons Winery
Roudon-Smith Vineyards
Santa Cruz Mountain
   Vineyard
Smothers Vine Hill Wines
F & M Steiger Winery
Sunrise Vineyards

Monterey

Carmel Bay Winery
Chalone Vineyard
Durney Vineyards
Jekel Vineyards
Monterey Peninsula Winery
River Run Vintners

Santa Barbara

Ballard Canyon Winery
Los Alamos Vineyards
Rancho Sisquoc Winery
Sanford & Benedict
  Vineyards
Santa Barbara Winery
Santa Ynez Valley Winery
The Vineyards at Zaca Mesa

Contra Costa

Digardi Winery
Viano Winery

San Benito

Calera Wine Company
Cygnet Cellars
Enz Vineyards
Hoffman Mountain Ranch
York Mountain Winery

Riverside

Callaway Vineyard

San Luis Obispo

Estrella River Vineyards
Las Tablas Winery
Mastantuono
Pesenti Winery

Sierra Foothills

Amador Winery
Argonaut Winery
Boeger Winery

Chispa Cellars
d'Agostini Winery
Eldorado Vineyards
Montevina
Shenandoah Vineyards
Sierra Vista Winery
Stevenot Winery
Stoneridge
Story Vineyard
Yankee Hill Winery

Livermore and Alameda

Concannon Vineyard
Villa Armando Winery
Weibel Champagne
  Vineyards
Wente Bros.

─── *AMERICAN WINES FROM COAST TO COAST* ───

California is far from the sole producer of American wines. There are new vineyards across the continent, mostly of local interest, but a few bottles reach major markets from New York, the Great Lakes, and the Northwest, the best of them from noble vines like Chardonnay and Riesling, Cabernet Sauvignon and Pinot Noir, although crosses with native grapes, usually called French-American hybrids, are producing some exciting wines. Whites include Seyval Blanc and Aurora, reds from Baco Noir and Chelois, Maréchal Foch and de Chaunac, Chancellor and Chambourcin. The Eighties will see many more.

─────────────── *New York* ───────────────

Whites are best, but red blends and hybrids that are tart and dry should be sought.
Hudson Valley and Long Island:
      Benmarl Vineyards
      Hargrave Vineyards
The Finger Lakes:
      Bully Hill Wine Company
      Gold Seal
      Great Western (Pleasant Valley Wine Company)
      Taylor Wine Company
      Vinifera Wine Cellars
      Widmer's Wine Cellars

─────────────── *New England* ───────────────

The first modern vineyards were planted in New Hampshire, but those along the southern coast produce the most interesting wines.
      Sakonnet Vineyards
      White Mountain Vineyards

---------------------- *Pennsylvania* ----------------------

There are vineyards along the Delaware, but most are concentrated in the northeast corner of the state, near Lake Erie.
>Conestoga Vineyard
>Mazza Vineyards
>Penn-Shore
>Pequea Valley Vineyards
>Presque Isle Wine Cellars

---------------------- *Mid-Atlantic* ----------------------

Newspaperman Philip Wagner was the first major experimenter with hybrids, and vines from his Boordy Vineyard now populate vineyards from Texas to Ontario.
>Boordy Vineyards
>Caroli Vineyards
>Meredyth Vineyards
>Montbray Wine Cellars

---------------------- *Ohio* ----------------------

Sparkling Catawba from Cincinnati vineyards planted by Nicholas Longworth made the fame of American wines before the Civil War, but after Prohibition about the only winery left was Meier's Wine Cellars. A new generation has established vineyards near the Greak Lake and along the Ohio.
>Cedar Hill Wine Company
>Chalet Debonne
>Grands Vins Vineyards
>Markko Vineyards

——————————— *Indiana* ———————————

Small experimental vineyards, including one on strip-mined land across the Ohio in Kentucky, have begun marketing a few wines.

Banholzer Wine Cellars
Cape Sandy Vineyards
Golden Rain Tree Winery
Oliver Wine Company
Possum Trot Farm
Swiss Valley Vineyards
Villa Medeo

——————————— *Michigan* ———————————

Like New York, the home of the Concord grapes for juice and jelly has gradually extended plantings of vinifera and hybrids, producing some good, sharp wines.

Bronte Winery
Boskydel
Fenn Valley Vineyard
Frontenac Vineyards
Lakeside Vineyard
St. Julian Winery
Tabor Hill Vineyard
Vendramino
Warner Vineyards

——————————— *Wisconsin* ———————————

Still mostly Concords and native grapes, a few vineyards of hybrids and vinifera have been established, but only one manages to send a few bottles out of the state.

Wollersheim Winery

————————————— *The Ozarks* —————————————

Early settlers along the Missouri planted many vines, most done in by Prohibition, but old wineries have been re-established and new ones founded.

Bardenheier's
Mount Bethel Cellar
Mount Pleasant Vineyard
Peaceful Bend Vineyard
Post Winery
Saint James Winery
Stolz Vineyards
Stone Hill Wine Company
Wiederkehr Wine Cellars

————————————— *The Northwest* —————————————

Washington and Oregon boast a climate closest to that of Europe, with as much sunlight, so that wines close to European styles can be made. Rieslings and Chardonnays are especially interesting, but red wines are beginning to attract fans.

————————————— *Oregon* —————————————

Amity Vineyards
Coury Vineyard
Eyrie Vineyards
Hillcrest Vineyard
Knudsen-Erath Winery
Oak Knoll
Ponzi Vineyards
Tualatin Vineyards

Washington

Associated Vintners
Bingen Wine Cellars
Hinzerling Vineyards
Preston Wine Cellars
Saint Michelle Vineyards
Salishan Vineyard
Vierthaler Winery

Canada

Ontario's Niagara Peninsula has been the orchard center of Canada, some of the vineyards lying almost as far south as Pennsylvania, but there are recent plantings in British Columbia valleys, particularly the Okanagan.

Andres Wines
Calona Winery
Casabello
Chateau Gai
Inniskillin
Jordan Wine Company
Saint Michelle of Victoria

BUYING AMERICAN WINES

• *How many wines do I need for a good range of California wines?*

You want examples of the different varieties and regions from the best winemakers—about 30.

• *How many bottles?*

That depends on how much you drink. Let's say you use two or three bottles a week, plus two or three bottles for a weekly dinner party. That would come to about 150 bottles a year, or about a dozen cases a year. If you bought an average of a case a month to replace what you drink, you would be well supplied. Average price might be $40, so you would spend about $500 a year.

● *Which wines would you start with?*

With those from Napa. I buy mixed cases, starting with The Christian Brothers and Louis Martini. I buy a mixed case from Parducci in Mendocino, and another from Fetzer or Weibel or Cresta Blanca. From Sonoma I would get Sebastiani, Pedroncelli, Korbel, and Sonoma Vineyards. From Livermore I'd get Concannon or Wente. From Monterey I'd get Mirassou, Paul Masson, and Monterey Vineyards. Actually, I would get a case from each.

● *You left out a lot of Napa wineries.*

I'd also get a case from Mondavi, from Beringer, from Beaulieu Vineyards, and from Sterling. And I'd get a mixed case of Almadén or Charles Krug or Inglenook. Also I would buy one mixed case of wines from the giants—all Zinfandel—from Gallo, Guild, Italian Swiss, Franzia, along with any others I could find.

● *That's at least twenty cases.*

You have to start somewhere.

● *Which varieties would you buy?*

Zinfandel and Petite Sirah, of course, Cabernet and either Pinot Noir or one of the Gamays. Sauvignon Blanc, naturally, even if it's called Fumé Blanc, and Chardonnay. I'd include Chenin Blanc or Johannisberg Riesling, French Colombard or Gewürztraminer. And Sylvaner, even when it's called Riesling, and whatever other varieties the winery specializes in, like Folle Blanche from Louis Martini or Aurora from Parducci. I would get pairs of some wines, or different vintages, or special bottlings. You have to be flexible.

● *What about the smaller wineries?*

You can't leave them out, even though the wines cost more, averaging $8 a bottle. I'd buy mixed cases by variety and pour them as a second bottle on special occasions. I'd get cases of Cabernet and Zinfandel or Pinot Noir, a case of Sauvignon Blancs and a case of Chardonnays.

●*Which wineries would you include?*

Heitz, Chappellet, and Freemark Abbey from Napa, of course; Mayacamas or Stony Hill, Burgess, Spring Mountain, Chateau Montelena, Caymus, Clos du Val, Stag's Leap, Phelps, if possible. There's Edmeades and Husch from Mendocino. There's Pedroncelli and Hanzell from Sonoma, and also Simi, Geyser Peak, Dry Creek, Buena Vista, Wildwood, Z-D, Souverain, Kenwood, Trentadue. Down south, Chalone, Ridge, and Bruce have to be included, and there's Firestone, Hoffman Mountain Ranch, San Martin. There are more, but you would be hard put to find twenty different ones outside of California.

●*All those names are bewildering.*

Just buy what you can find, whenever you can find them. The wines are good, exciting, often superb. They're not to be missed, worth a detour, three stars.

●*How do I store them?*

These are wines for current drinking, to be drunk up within a year, so they can go in a closet that doesn't get too warm, where they won't be subject to vibration or light. Cool storage in a cellar is best, where the wines will be kept at earth temperature, around 12° Celsius, that's about 55° Fahrenheit. An even temperature is best.

●*What about Eastern wines?*

You can hunt for Chelois, Maréchal Foch, Baco Noir for reds, Chardonnay or Delaware for whites. You shouldn't miss bottles from Konstantin Frank's Vinifera Wine Cellars, Boordy Vineyard, Bully Hill, Gold Seal, Widmer, Benmarl. Good bottles come from Pennsylvania, Maryland, Arkansas, Michigan, Canada's Niagara Peninsula, Ohio, Missouri, almost every state, but they are impossible to find. The best of all may come from Hargraves Vineyard, out on Long Island, but who can find them?

———12 SOURCES FOR HOME VINEYARDS:——— GRAFTED VINES AND ROOTSTOCKS

Alpine Nursery, Altus, Arkansas 72821

Armstrong Nurseries, Ontario, California 91761

Boordy Vineyards, Riderwood, Maryland 21139

Bully Hill Vineyards, Hammondsport, New York 14840

California Nursery Company, Fremont, California 94536

Cal-Western Nurseries, Visalia, California 93277

Chicama Vineyards, Vineyard Haven, Massachusetts 02568

Foundation Plant Material Service, Davis, California 95616

Dr. Konstantin Frank, Hammondsport, New York 14840

The Grafted Grape Nursery, Clifton Springs, New York 14432

John W. Moorhead, North East, Pennsylvania 16428

New York State Fruit Testing Cooperative, Geneva, New York 14456

Many vineyards and most nurseries offer vines adapted to local soils and climates, and they will provide information on tending.

● *What about the Pacific Northwest?*
    Saint Michelle is the only one occasionally available, but there are going to be wonders. American wines have scarcely begun to appear around the country. It's a new world to explore.

●*How do you serve these wines?*

Half a bottle at a time, when I'm organized. At a dinner party I like to taste two or three different wines, a glass or two of each, maybe. I have a case of empty half-bottles with screw tops. When I open a bottle, I fill one of the half-bottles and label it, then put what's left of the full bottle on the table for drinking. If one of them is irresistible, I dig out the half-bottle I've set aside.

●*How much wine do you pour in each glass?*

Normally, a bottle will serve four people twice, at about 3 ounces per glass. If we're serving several wines, I often make a half-bottle serve the number of guests, which is rarely more than six. I like to serve a jug wine to start, or an ordinary, inexpensive one. I'll pour other wines when people want to taste, which is only once in a while. Often they just want to have dinner and talk. When that's the case, I usually open a sweet wine for dessert, to have with fruit. We use a lot of glasses, but not always that much wine, perhaps two or three bottles at a dinner party. Any left over goes for cooking.

——————————— *BUYING JUG WINES* ———————————

There used to be gallon bottles of wine, but these were too bulky; then there were half-gallons, but these were too tall to go into the refrigerator. No longer. Now there are metric sizes of 1 liter, 1½ liters, and 3 liters; the jug isn't what it was. The double bottle, the magnum, was once reserved for only the best wines, but now low-priced wines come in double bottles, as well as in all the metric sizes. You have to watch out to be sure you are getting your money's worth.

The popular jug size these days is 1.5 liters or 50.7 ounces, the traditional magnum. When you pay $4 dollars for one, you are paying the equivalent of $2.65 a bottle, which is a high price for a cheap wine. Jug wines are no longer that cheap, but of course the wine is better than it was a decade ago.

Most jug wines come from regions of large production where there is plenty of wine to make the blends: for instance, Italy, Spain, California, Bordeaux, and the Rhône. They are sold mostly by brand name and they vary widely. A brand may be dry one shipment, fruity the next, bland the one after that, depending on available stocks or the whim of the shipper. If a successful brand is a little sweet, other shippers will copy it.

The best way to buy jug wines is to try any new ones on the market, switching when they pall or when the wine changes. New brands are usually good wines, the prices set low to attract buyers; when the wine finds an audience, prices rise.

Explanations don't satisfy someone who wants a name to ask for in a shop. Here are names of some shippers who sell much wine in this country, have a reputation to protect, and have an ever larger market to appeal to. Most shippers offer red and white wines.

Italy

Italian jugs are generally pleasant, somewhat dry, often fruity, too often bland. Look particularly for wines from cooperatives, or Cantinas Sociales, such as Riunite.

Segesta, from Sicily
Marino, wines from the Roman Hills, Castelli Romani
Colli Albani, wines from the Roman Hills
Riunite, wines from Reggio Emilia
Ristoro, from northern vineyards

NOTE: *The most popular Italian wines, Chianti, Soave, Valpolicella, and Bardolino, are marketed in large bottles. The following are widely distributed:*

Antinori	Frescobaldi
Bertani	Lamberti
Bolla	Opici
Cella	Ruffino
Folonari	Villa Banfi

———————————— Spain ————————————

Spanish jug wines can be fresh, fruity, and easy to drink, but are often bland, sometimes harsh.

Juan Hernández, from Valencia
Yago, bottled in Rioja
AGE, bottled in Rioja
Cepa Negra, from Barcelona

———————————— France ————————————

The French customarily bottle some of their wines in magnums, usually the best of them because the wines mature more slowly in the big bottles. Those that qualify as jug wines are $5 or so, most of them from the big shippers of Bordeaux and the Rhône. The wines are generally in the traditional styles, ranging from dry to fruity.

Côteaux du Languedoc, George Bonfils
de Luze Club Claret
Pierre Cartier
Ecu Royale
Victori
Chapoutier

California

Most nationally distributed shippers market generic wines—burgundy, etc.—in large bottles; several offer varietals, particularly Zinfandel. A type identified as "Mellow" on the label is usually somewhat sweet; those called "Mountain" are usually dry. Look for those under $5 from Napa, Sonoma, and Mendocino, Santa Clara and San Luis Obispo, Monterey and Santa Barbara. Try the following:

> Robert Mondavi: reds and whites
> Louis Martini: Mountain Red, Barbera
> The Christian Brothers: Claret and Chablis
> Charles Krug: particularly for whites
> Sebastiani: particularly for reds
> Inglenook: Zinfandel
> Villa Armando: particularly for reds
> Almadén: Mountain Red and Grenache Rosé
> Paul Masson: Rhine Wine, Baroque

CLIFFDWELLER WINES

Apartments are fine places to keep wines—for a month or so, from one season to the next, but not much longer. The change from winter to summer and back to winter again quickly ages wines, as does the day to night change of temperature and vibration from tramping feet and rumbling vehicles.

Wines that have to be kept for years to mature rarely develop well when temperatures reach the 70's; the best temperature is a constant 50°F or so, perhaps 10° or 12° Celsius, in a cellar that is dark and somewhat damp. Fortunately, wines are sturdy, especially when they have 12 percent or more alcohol, and although they age faster in warm surroundings, they bear up. Temperature change and vibration do them in, however.

A seldom-used closet, if there is such a thing in an apartment, is good storage space because all the other things tucked away there act as insulation. The best containers are partitioned cartons laid on their sides, the corrugated paper providing a little more insulation. No matter where they live, most people buy wines for drinking within a month or so and all the fuss about proper care scarcely matters. Few people with cellars buy wine for drinking in the next decade, so apartment dwellers need not feel shut off from the good things of life. Wine shops will often store wines for a small fee per year for those who want to make sure they have old wines for drinking in the Nineties.

Not being able to store wines can be an advantage in times of inflation, for wine prices fluctuate. There are exceptions. The '74 Bordeaux, for example, a bargain at the beginning of the Eighties, were priced below the expensive '73s and the scarce and expensive '75s and '76s. The '74 vintage won't be at its best until the middle Eighties, and is well worth storing in a closet for a couple of years, and will continue to be when priced below the other vintages. Much the same consideration goes for wines overshadowed by famous neighbors, like Hermitage and Côte Rôtie of the Rhône, which are passed over in favor of Burgundies or Châteauneuf-du-Pape. And some wines that take years to develop are simply unknown, but worth keeping because they are low in price; wines like Cahors, or wines of the Italian Piedmont, or the Riservas of Rioja are worth taking a chance on. California Cabernets, although famous and high in price, mature more quickly than their European peers and are sturdy enough to live through a couple of closet winters. Saint Emilions, Pomerols, and the lesser wines of Bordeaux are worth taking a chance on.

Only the greatest wines require perfect storage, just because they can be so superb when well cared for.

Because most of us are content with wines that are ready to drink five years after vintage, or sooner, space is the only real problem. Most overstuffed closets can handle four cases of wine, stacked way back in the corner. A kitchen cabinet, a bureau drawer, or a wine rack behind the sofa will do well by wines that will be drunk in a matter of weeks. Most of us can find room in the refrigerator for a bottle or two of white wine or Champagne; a couple of weeks in the cold won't hurt the wine a bit.

Although apartments are not good places for storing the best wines, they are fine places in which to let a good wine rest, for the week or two needed for the wine to settle down after its trip from the store. A few minutes of joggling will put a wine out of shape for days, a fact few believe. Test for yourself, by buying a bottle of the same wine that has rested for a week or two, then opening them together. The wine that has rested will be noticeably better. An apartment is a good place for such experiment, over and over again.

———— NEWSLETTERS—A FEW OF THE BEST ————

Scores of vineyards send out news and notices about new wines. Your favorites are often glad to put you on their mailing lists. However, because mailing has become expensive, they are quick to drop you if you fail to order. Several vineyards issue newsletters every month or so. Among them are:

Bottles and Bins, the first of the newsletters, written for more than 25 years by Francis L. Gould. Chatty, cheerful, and full of recipes from readers. Address: P.O. Box 191, St. Helena, Calif. 94574.

Inglenook Notes, mostly concerned with new wines, from one of the Napa Valley's first vineyards. Address: 601 4th St., San Francisco, Calif. 94107.

Latest Press, filled with information about winemaking, with recipes from members of the large Mirassou clan. Address: 3000 Aborn Rd., San Jose, Calif. 94121.

LOWER-CASE WINES

Just as the English created the modern world of wines by making a market for them, so they created a wine language, intended to simplify, but ultimately confusing.

Certain words quickly become common currency in the English language: macintosh and macadam, sandwich and blucher, raglan and burberry, the names of men who made things new. Victorian dieters said they were banting, a term named after the man who found you could lose weight by eating meat. A similar approach was used in naming wines:

hock: German white wine, after Hochheim, the town at the east end of the greatest German district, the Rheingau.

claret: Bordeaux red wine, after the name of a light, pale red called *clairet*.

sherry: The fortified wines of Spain, produced around Jerez de la Frontera, first called "Jerries", by stevedores, then later corrupted still more. Originally, sherries were called "sack" because the casts were marked *secco*, the Spanish word for dry.

port: The red fortified wine of Portugal, named after the town from which it was shipped, Oporto.

burgundy: The reds of the Côte d'Or and vineyards south down the Rhône, a corruption of Bourgogne, the ancient duchy.

champagne: The sparkling wine from that region east of Paris, once sweet, but made dry for the Edwardians, who gave it pet names, such as The Bubbly, champs, tiddly, and worse. Veuve Clicquot is called The Widow; Charles Heidsieck is called Charlie; Piper-Heidsieck is called The Piper (or pee-pair, if you are being la-dee-dah). Many of the houses are known by the first parts of their names: Moët, Perrier. Irroy is sometimes called Ip Ip.

Anglicizing of continental names maddened producers, who felt they were really geographical and unique, that no other sparkling wine was like Champagne, no other reds were like those of Bourgogne. The best practice is to spell the word Sherry when you mean the wine of Spain, Port when you mean the wine of Portugal, Champagne when you mean the wine from that district. Nothing is to be done about hock or claret. Now, what do you make of Wisconsin Swiss cheese? Or georgia peaches?

News from the Peak, a well-written report on Russian River activities, with notes from the winemaker. Address: 4340 Redwood Highway, Suite 220, San Rafael, Calif. 94903.

Papagni Press, with notes on more than vineyard activities, including Papagni family recipes and notes on unusual wines. Address: 31754 Avenue 9, Madeira, Calif. 93637.

Sebastiani Vineyards, with excellent accounts of vineyard activities, some of the best recipes from the family collection, and a running journal of the family bird sanctuary. Address: P.O. Box AA, Sonoma, Calif. 95476.

Vineyard Vignettes, with notes about experimental wines and family recipes. Address: Concannon Vineyard, Box 432, Livermore, Calif. 94550.

Winemasters' News grew from a regular press release to its present form, with recipes and accounts of developments from one of the largest producers. Address: Guild Wineries, 500 Sansome St., San Francisco, Calif. 94111.

The Woodinville Press, from Washington's leading producer, full of detailed reports of the new wines from the best of the country's new regions. Address: Chateau Sainte Michelle, Box 1976, Woodinville, WA. 98072.

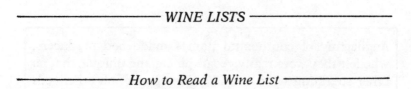

————————— *How to Read a Wine List* —————————

Wines are expensive in restaurants, where mark-ups are at least twice their cost, so the problem in ordering a wine is to find good bottles that are not exorbitant. Famous wines, fashionable ones, and older vintages are apt to be outrageous. To make some sense of pricing, you should know the cost of a few wines in a wine shop—a good Beaujolais growth, for instance, or a Muscadet, or Liebfraumilch. If prices for wines available in quantity are high, prices for wines limited in quantity can be astronomic.

Always ask for suggestions from the captain or owner, not from the waiter. Restaurants buy wines at the same prices as do wine shops, getting discounts when they buy 10 cases, or 50, and the savings may be reflected in the prices. Importers like restaurants that feature their wines, frequently offering them special bottlings and special prices. In a good restaurant the suggested wine is usually the best buy. If the bottle is unsatisfactory, change restaurants.

Before ordering any wine, look around at the other tables. If there are bottles on most of them, you can order with some assurance. If nobody else is drinking wine, consider beer.

Poring over the wine list is considered bad form in gastronomic circles. It is proper to leaf through a list to see what's there, but prolonged study or cross-questioning of staff is pretentious.

The most revealing section of any wine list is usually Burgundy. It pays to know one of the Burgundy districts fairly well—Chablis, for instance, or Nuits Saint Georges, or Beaune. If there are several First Growths, at least some estate-bottlings, and a representation of wines from good shippers, chances are fair to good that other regions will be adequately represented.

A good restaurant wine list will offer several inexpensive wines from shippers with good reputations. There should be an Alsatian Sylvaner, a Côtes-du-Rhône, a Rioja, a Kabinett from the Rhine, a Chianti or Valpolicella or Soave, all priced at well below $10. You should be able to find a Mâcon Blanc or Blanc de Blancs, a Saint Emilion or Petit Château of Bordeaux at similar prices.

Every good restaurant in this country should have a representative selection of California wines. Even good French and Italian restaurants, except those incorrigibly provincial and chauvinistic, will offer a good Chardonnay or Cabernet and a carafe wine from a good shipper. Presence on a list of Louis Martini, Wente, Beaulieu Vineyards, Sebastiani, The Christian Brothers, or Monterey Vineyards—at least one of these—is a good sign that the restaurant knows good and reasonable wines. If none of the above appears, then such popular producers as Paul Masson, Almadén, or Inglenook should be represented.

Check the list of Champagnes. There should be several famous brands offered at well under $20.

Restaurants that pride themselves on their wines will offer a short list of 50 selections or so. (Some restaurants restrict themselves to about a dozen, usually well selected, not wishing to tie up money in extensive inventory.) Such lists can be considered at a glance, with some confidence that the restaurant sells the wines in quantity and keeps them well stocked.

Ornate wine lists are no sign of excellence, particularly if many items are crossed out. Often enough, the restaurant will not cross out items no longer stocked; if your first two choices are not available, consider beer. My favorite lists are those that contain labels so I can recognize those that

I like, even when the names slip my mind. Some consider these pretentious; I consider them to be clear, open, and practical. Remember, however, that you can't tell a wine list by its cover.

Do not be surprised when prices vary from one restaurant to another, particularly for older wines. A restaurant that buys wine when it is first offered on the market will pay less than a restaurant that buys a vintage after it becomes scarce. Some restaurants sell wines at a markup based on original purchase price; others mark up old bottles 10 percent for each year they hold them. Both practices are reasonable. Bear in mind that a new restaurant must pay high prices for old vintages, while an old restaurant may have extensive stocks that have been held for years.

Check the wine list. Trust the restaurateur. If you are disappointed, cross the restaurant off your list.

──────── *Ten Ways to Tell a Good Wine List* ────────

1. It has many wines under $10, several under $5.

2. There is a generous selection of half-bottles.

3. List is clean, not too long, clearly divided into country and region.

4. Only a few items are crossed out.

5. Vintages are listed for every wine, or NV indicated.

6. There is a long list of California wines from Napa, Sonoma, Mendocino, Monterey, and others.

7. Bordeaux list includes Saint Emilions, Pomerols, Graves, and several Petits Châteaux—five years or older.

8. Burgundy list includes Beaujolais growths and several estate-bottlings.

9. Rhine wines include QbA and Kabinett listings.

10. There are listed some unusual Italian wines, Spanish Riojas, and at least a few from other countries and regions.

Ten Ways to Tell a Poor Wine List

1. List is dirty, stained, or dilapidated—but if it is only well thumbed, that's a good sign.

2. Burgundies listed are only those with commune or town names—no estate-bottlings—and bottlings from little-known shippers.

3. Wines are listed without vintages.

4. Many items are crossed out.

5. Higher prices are inked in.

6. There is more than one misspelling.

7. There is only a short list of California wines, most of them from bulk shippers in San Joaquin valley.

8. Italian wines are limited to Chianti, Bardolino, Valpolicella, and Soave.

9. Rhine wines consist mostly of Liebfraumilch, Moselblümchen, Zeller Schwarze Katz, and Kröver Nacktarsch.

10. There are only a couple of wines under $5, most being over $10.

New York's Best Wine Lists

New York was the world's greatest wine town when the Seventies began. London had its Ports and old clarets, Paris had the range, but New York had all the great wines, and all the vintages from the Forties on, because the dollar was strong and the best restaurants were French, both in the kitchens and in the cellars. Even hotels had spectacular lists, particularly the St. Regis and the Waldorf. French bistros off Broadway near the French Line piers had unbelievable Burgundies, and all the East Side places spawned by Henri Soulé's Pavillon offered clarets and Burgundies for $10 that were unobtainable in Paris.

Most of the wines—and the cellars—were gone by the

beginning of the Eighties. Most of the wines had been drunk and not replaced. In 1970, a hundred thousand dollars would provide a restaurant with a superb cellar. Today, a quarter of a million dollars would be needed, and the wines are simply not available; demand for the limited supply has spread beyond Europe as far as Japan. There are many good wines around, some of them reasonable, but most restaurants and hotels are content to serve shippers' wines. Listed here are the best cellars in town, now few in number:

Lutèce
The Four Seasons
Windows on the World
Hotel Carlyle
The Coach House
Maxwell's Plum
Gian Marino
Barbetta Restaurant
Sparks Steak House
Claret's
The Caliban

NOTE: Many restaurants still have bottles tucked away, most easily discovered by talking to the wine steward or owner; good bets are 21 and Le Chambertin, whose once fabulous cellars are sadly depleted. Rumors from the hinterlands indicate that superior wines can be found at Hubert's in Brooklyn, at the Quay in Sea Bright, New Jersey. Out on Long Island, two notable places are Zanghi's in Glen Cove and Squire's in East Hampton.

——————— *California's Best Wine Lists* ———————

California's wine consumption is twice that of New York's—together they account for a third of all the wines drunk in the country—and there are many excellent wine lists, a few of which are listed below. One of the most selective, with many old bottles, is that of the Imperial Dynasty, in Hanford, near Fresno. This restaurant is worth a special trip; it's one of the best in the country.

> Clift Hotel, at Geary and Taylor Streets, San Francisco
>
> Stanford Court Hotel, 905 California Street, San Francisco
>
> Canlis' Restaurant, at California and Mason Streets, San Francisco
>
> Rolf's Restaurant, 757 Beach, San Francisco
>
> The North Beach, 1312 Stockton, San Francisco
>
> Pip's, 828 South Robertson Boulevard, Los Angeles
>
> Industry Hills Exhibit Center, City of Industry, near Los Angeles
>
> Wally's Desert Turtle, 71-775 Highway 111, Rancho Mirage, near Palm Springs
>
> Domaine Chandon, California Drive, Yountville (Napa Valley)
>
> Silverado Restaurant, 1374 Lincoln Avenue, Calistoga (Napa Valley)
>
> Au Relais, 691 Broadway, Sonoma

——— PRONOUNCING WINE WORDS ———

American tongues that can't roll an *r* or growl a gutteral are able to pronounce wine words well enough to be understood, and that's all that's necessary. The difference between *pwee-yee fwee-say and pooy-ye fwee-say* has not prevented Pouilly-Fuissé from becoming one of the most popular of dry white wines. A generation ago the trade said you couldn't sell it because nobody could pronounce it; now they say it sells so well because it's easy to say. Some people call it *pooly-foosy,* which is wrong, but they manage to get the wine. The French sound every syllable, stressing only lightly, but there are a lot of silent letters or half-silent letters and variants of sound for the same letters, just as in English. German is worse, or better, depending on which language you favor, as are Italian, Spanish, and Portuguese. Phonetics don't help much and are usually just funny.

Vin is *van*, not *vann* or *vin;* and *vino* is *VEE-no*, not *vie-no*. Most people say these right. But Montrachet is *mawn-rah-shay* and most people say it wrong. It's *REES-ling*, not *RICE-ling;* it's *sil-VAN-er* in Germany, *seel-vah-nair* in Alsace, and sometimes *SIL-van-er* in California. Saying things wrong bothers some people, others rise above it. Most of us do the best we can.

Is it helpful to know that Beaujolais-Villages is pronounced *bo-jo-lay vee-lahj?* Even that's not quite right. The *j* is sort of *szh* and the *g* is sort of *zsh*. The double *l* of village does not have the *yuh* sound, as it does in so many French words, but is a very definite *l* as in "follow," and not many French speakers can tell you why.

Pronouncing foreign words wrong is the only way for most of us. When somebody corrects you it is usually a put-down, a sign of bad manners on their part, unpleasant all around. Pronounciation changes from generation to generation, anyway, so we all might as well enjoy trying to say some of those outlandish words that can stand for perfectly splendid wines.

Chablis is *shab-lee*, Chambertin is *shawm-bare-tan* (go easy on the *m* and *n*), and Champagne is *shawm-pahn-yuh*, but it's also *sham-PANE*. Also, that *shawm* is just as often *shahm*. One of my favorites is the sweet Bordeaux, Sainte-Croix-du-Mont, *sant-crwa-dew-mawn*. Another is Manzanilla, *mahn-thah-NEEL-yah*. A third is Vinho Verde, *VEEN-ho VARE-dzh*. The names are okay, but what I like about them is that all three are bargains, worth getting, no matter what you say.

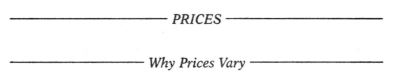

PRICES

Why Prices Vary

When somebody asks why a case of wine costs so much, you might like to have a ready answer. A wine costing $6 in New York may cost $8 in Chicago, $10 in Kansas City, $5 in Dallas, $10 in Denver, and $7 in San Francisco—and all the prices are fair. Shipping, local taxes, the quantity of wine sold in the market, the number of distribution channels it goes through, all govern the price of the bottle on the shelf.

Let's say a case of wine costs $12 abroad. That price includes bottling and packing charges, shipment to a port, and profit for the shipper, all of which may amount to half this cost. Ocean freight, insurance, warehousing, and import duties may add on $6. The importer may be content with a profit of one-third, which includes the cost of advertising, salesmen on the road, overhead, and what-not. The case of wine now costs $24.

A distributor may content himself with a profit of 25 percent, so the cost to the retailer becomes $30. If he is content with a 50 percent markup, the wine will cost a customer $45 for a case of twelve bottles plus sales tax, or close to $4 a bottle.

A few charges may have been left out: trucking within the country or charges for interest on money borrowed to buy the wine, for example. The wine may go through an additional step in the chain, from importer to wholesaler to distributor to retailer. This is customery for anything sold, as we all understand quite well, but people are forever asking why wine costs so much.

The chain of sale is often bypassed by a major retailer who sells a lot of wine. He may buy a hundred cases for a lower price than your friendly neighborhood shop that buys a case at a time. A retailer in a major market may buy an entire container of a thousand or more cases direct from the importer. He may even buy direct from the shipper of the wine, a practice called Direct Import, DI for short. A store that does this is worth looking for.

National brands are quite a different matter; they cost about the same everywhere. An importer may need 50,000 cases of a wine for national distribution, so his interest in small lots is minimal. But even with so much wine, he may be able to concentrate only on major markets. That is why many good-sized cities may not have some of the advertised brands; bigger cities take it all. Among major importers there is not much talk of expanding markets these days; somebody has figured that it costs a thousand dollars a week to keep a salesman on the road.

————————— *What to Do About High Prices* —————————

Women buy more wine than men, and that's a blessing. Women read ads, know how to shop (they take time to see what's there, they ask questions, they are leery of sales pitches); they compare prices, try different stores. Some men do the same, even make a study of wines, but they are more apt to latch onto a couple of names, spend an extra dollar when touted, and complain a lot when the wine doesn't measure up. There are too many wines at too many prices for most people, so they settle for whatever is moving in their friendly neighborhood store.

Variety is the nature of wines. That may be the secret to finding bargains. Find a wine you like, then buy a case. Find a second wine you like and buy a second case. Buying brands and famous names is a sure way to shut out other wines from the market. Your friendly neighborhood store may offer nothing else. For bargains you have to shop in stores that sell lots of wines; take a chance and buy those you never heard of.

There's no rule of thumb for telling when a wine is too high in price. Once you are past brands and famous names there's a jungle to explore. For wines under $5 you just have to look around for unknowns. If local stocks are limited, take a trip to Washington, Boston, New York, Chicago, Denver, Dallas, San Francisco. Buy mixed cases whenever you are near a wine shop.

Get to know some price ranges. When Côte-du-Rhônes are less than Bordeaux Supérieur, buy them—but switch when the prices reverse. When Spanish Riojas are less than Italian wines of the Piedmont, lay in a stock. Try Zinfandel or Petite Sirah from California—not just one but several, at various prices. Try California Cabernets in the same price brackets as Bordeaux Châteaux; the wines are different, but both are good and there are satisfying similarities. There is a tremendous variety of wines selling under $10, which is considered a reasonable price for a good bottle these days; by the end of the decade they will have gone up half again, or doubled.

Check price ranges in May and June, again in January and February. New wines arriving in the spring force odds and ends off the shelves. There are always sales after the first of the year, before inventories are taken. Knowing sale prices helps you find bargains at other times of the year.

A good bottle of wine costs less than a steak or a pair of tickets to a movie or concert, which is a matter of surprise to those who think a $10 bottle is a rip-off. There are wines worth more, but those are extravagances, for special occasions like the first day of spring or when you get a haircut.

Ten dollars can get you hundreds of the world's best wines. They won't be the best known, nor will they be particularly rare, like estate-bottled Burgundies or Classed Growths of Bordeaux, although you may even find some of these. They may come from a small producer somebody has sought out; there may be only a few hundred cases for the market, perhaps limited to a single store. But these are the wines to look for, $10 bargains nobody knows, and some of them are half that. They have to be looked for, tasted, and remembered so that you can buy a case. Some of the best wines are lost because the name has been forgotten.

Knowing prices helps, but taste tells. The best wines on the market have to be discovered. Consider taking a look tomorrow.

———————— *Burgundy Prices a Generation Ago* ————————

The last of the wine shops catering to the carriage trade, M. Lehmann of Park Avenue, 25 years ago offered estate-bottlings from a dozen of Burgundy's most illustrious growers. Wines mostly of the fabled 1953 vintage were offered at low prices, just before arrival. Here is a selection from that list, prices for a case of twelve bottles, rounded to the nearest dollar:

Robert Vocoret: Chablis La Forêt	$35
Pierre Gelin: Fixin Clos du Chapitre	27
Hippolyte Ponsot: Clos de la Roche	43
Gustave Gros: Richebourg	59
Henri Lamarche: Vosne-Romanée Malconsorts	48
Jean Mongeard: Grands Echézeaux	48
Emile Mugneret: Echézeaux	39
Henri Gouges: Les Porrets '52	37
Maurice Drouhin: Clos Vougeot '52	49
Marquis d 'Angerville: Volnay Clos des Champans	35
Edouard Deleger: Chevalier-Montrachet	44
Edmond Laneyrie: Pouilly-Fuissé	25

These were opening prices in 1955. Two years later, they were half again as much; they had doubled by 1960.

--- *Paris Prices* ---

The French were drinking brand names as prices doubled during the Seventies. As world demand continues for famous French wines, the French will be drinking less and less of them—and paying as much as New Yorkers do. Nicolas, the largest of the French chains of wine shops, was offering their own brands of VDQS wines at the equivalent of nearly $2 a bottle with the advent of the Eighties. Prices were rising:

Bourgogne 1977

Mercurey	6.25
Savigny	7.00
Morey St. Denis	8.75
Gevrey Chambertin	10.00
Aloxe Corton	11.25
Bordeaux NV	2.75
Médoc NV	3.75
Saint Estèphe NV	4.50
Saint Emilion NV	4.75
Côtes-du-Rhône-Villages	3.50

Loire 1977

Sancerre	6.00
Saint Nicolas	3.50
Vouvray	3.25

NOTE: Prices based on 4 francs to the dollar, rounded off.

4.
Tasting

DRINKING NEW WINES

Vintners used to hang a bush above the door when the new wine was ready, not always to public joy, for the custom provoked the adage, "A good wine needs no bush." New wines today are heralded by state fair judgings, wine queens on TV, vintage hot lines, press junkets, wine society dinners, jingles, T-shirt giveaways, even ads. You can't tell a wine by its hullabaloo.

The fun begins in mid-November, when Beaujolais Nouveau arrives in Paris, more to start talk than to give an idea of what the new vintage is like. By Christmas, bottles have been flown to the big cities and soon Beaujolais more completely vinified appears. By spring, a host of whites—Muscadet, Frascati, Rhenish Tafelwein—are available for the

Easter ham. Rosés appear for the summer, light reds from Mediterranean vineyards for autumn, and then Beaujolais Nouveau again. All give hints about a quite different sort of wine—those that develop in cask and must spend time in bottle before reaching maturity.

Precocious wines—reds like Beaujolais, rosés, all but the greatest whites—are best drunk young, within a year or two of the vintage. Quickly ready, they need little time in cask, or none; they are bottled only as a convenience to get them to market.

Early wines—reds like Côte-du-Rhône or Bardolino—need a few months in cask to lose roughness. At their best in the second or third year, they lose freshness and quickly fade.

Late bloomers—Burgundy reds and those from Italy's Piedmont—need six months to a year in cask, to round out. The best of them need longer and a great Bordeaux may rest thirty months in wood: once bottled, such a wine may need years in glass to become ready for drinking. Many are too young five years after the vintage, as are great sweet wines like Sauternes or German Auslesen.

Following is a schedule of wines that need time to develop, with indications of when they are first ready for tasting.

● *After 2 years*

All regional whites:

Soave, Verdicchio, Pinot Grigio, etc., from Italy.

QbA, Liebfraumilch, Frankenwein, etc., from Germany.

Sancerre, Pouilly-Fumé, etc., from Loire.

Mâcon Blanc, Chablis, Montagny, etc., from Burgundy.

Light regional reds:

Bardolino, Valpolicella, Chianti, etc., from Italy.

Chinon, Champigny, Bourgueil, etc., from Loire. Côtes-du-Rhône, Mâcon Rouge.

Valdepeñas and Panadés from Spain.

All rosés.

California varietals: Chenin Blanc, Sylvaner, French Colombard.

● *After 3 years*

Burgundy whites: Chablis Premier Cru and Grand Cru, Meursault, Puligny-Montrachet, Chassagne-Montrachet, Pouilly-Fuissé.

Bordeaux whites: Entre-Deux-Mers, Graves Supérieur, Sauternes.

Rhine whites: Kabinett, Spätlese, Auslese.

Côte de Beaune reds: Volnay, Beaune, Pommard, etc.

Bordeaux Rouge, Bordeaux Supérieur

California varietals: Zinfandel, Gamay Beaujolais, Napa Gamay, Barbera, Sauvignon Blanc, Semillon.

Italian reds: Chianti Riserva, Valpolicella Superiore, Nebbiolo or Spanna, Freisa, Grignolino.

All VDQS wines from France.

● *After 4 years*

Burgundy Premier Cru and Grand Cru.

Bordeaux Petits Châteaux and district wines: Médoc, Margaux, Saint Julien, Saint Estèphe, Saint Emilion, Montagne-Saint Emilion, etc. Pomerol, Lalande de Pomerol. Graves. Côtes Canon Fronsac.

Côte Rôtie, Hermitage, Crozes-Hermitage, Châteauneuf-du-Pape, from Rhône.

Gattinara, Barolo, Barbaresco, Valtellina, Brunello, from Italy.

Rioja Reserva, from Spain.

California varietals: Cabernet Sauvignon, Merlot, Pinot Noir, Chardonnay, White Riesling.

● *After 5 years*

Bordeaux Cru Classé.

● *After 10 years*

Bordeaux Premier Grand Cru Classé.

● *After 20 years*

Vintage Port.

● *After 30 years*

Tokay Eszencia.

DRINKING OLD VINTAGES

Wine is grape juice on the way to vinegar, so the saw goes, and few of us get to taste old wines that are still sound. A wine has to be kept well if it is to have a long life, in a cellar, cool, dark, and still. A great wine is often defined as one that not only is typical of the region and grape from which it comes, but that lives a long time. A long time for most great wines is twenty years, even when the vintage is outstanding.

Claret lovers with wise parents or great perspicacity, or both, are drinking their '53s and '55s, their fading '59s and perfect '62s, opening the last of their '49s and '45s, looking ahead to the '66s and '64s, and trying to restrain themselves so that their offspring will drink the '61s.

Burgundy lovers are treasuring the last of the '61s and the '55s, are drinking the '64s, '66s, and '70s, and are looking forward to the '73s, '72s, '71s, and '69s, in that order.

But we are talking only about the greatest wines—and about wines that were bought when they first came on the market, were stored in a cool cellar, and were never moved.

If the cellar was truly cool (50°F or 10°C) and somewhat damp, then even great dry white wines will have lasted, along with the Sauternes and the Auslesen.

The bottles are brought up a couple of days before they are to be served and stood up in a corner of the dining room, which is also a cool 68°F or 10°C.

The corks are pulled as the wines are drunk; the wine is decanted, if necessary, and poured for each guest. If the wine needs time to aerate—buffs say the wines need to breathe—the guests swirl their glasses and wait while the wine opens up. Sometimes only the first sip retains its wonder, sometimes the wine will take an hour to reveal itself. And a wine will vary from bottle to bottle, a magnum opening up more slowly than a standard bottle.

To drink a perfect old wine, perhaps only once or

twice in a lifetime, is to experience one of life's rarest delights
Here are some of them:

    Bordeaux: '20 & '21, '28 & '29, '34 & '37, '42 & '43, '45
      & '47 & '49

    Burgundy: '28 & '29, '33 & '34, '37, '42 & '43, '45 & '47
      & '49

    Champagne: '28 & '29, '33 & '37, '42 & '43, '45 & '47 &
      '49

    Porto: '20 & '22, '24 & '27, '34 & '35, '42 & '45, '48 &
      '50

NOTE: Sweet wines like the Sauternes of Bordeaux and the Auslesen of the Rhine become intense and tonic after twenty years; many of them are exciting to drink when half a century or more old. Vouvray of a great year can last as long, as do the Anjou wines of Quarts de Chaume and Bonnezeaux. A wine like Tokay never seems to die.

——— *A NICE LITTLE WINE BEFORE DINNER...* ———

The fashion of drinking wine before dinner is a trend that will burgeon in the Eighties because of the general feeling that wine is light and easy, and low in calories. The usual serving is 3 ounces, a glass containing about as much alcohol as a highball.*

Those who drink two or three glasses of wine before dinner are not consuming very many calories but are taking in a lot of fruit acids, which can be distressing to an empty stomach. Soft white wines light in body are the easiest to drink and the list is long.

> **A highball made with a jigger—perhaps an ounce—of 86 proof spirits contains about that many calories. Proof is twice the percentage of alcohol; table wines average about 12 percent alcohol, or 24 proof, or about 72 calories per 3-ounce glass.*

> *Those who drink beer will think beer.*
> Washington Irving

---------------- *Soft White Wines* ----------------

• *Rhine wines* Those from the Rheinhessen, Rheinpfalz, Franconia, Baden. (Moselle wines are light alcohol but often dry and hard; those from the Rheingau are full and fruity.)

• *Italian wines* Most of them are soft and light in acid, particularly from Soave, Cortese, Frascati, Orvieto, and Pinot Grigio. (Verdicchio, Caldaro, Verdiso, and Lacrima Christi can range from light to fruity.)

• *French wines* Graves from Bordeaux, Vouvray from the Loire, Sylvaner from Alsace. (Entre-Deux-Mers, once soft, is now mostly dry, as are white Burgundies and those from the Loire, like Muscadet and Sancerre; dry wines are the French preference.)

• *California wines* Sauvignon Blanc, White Riesling, Chenin Blanc, usually dry; Chardonnay, usually dry and fruity.

White wines are generally preferred over reds to drink as aperitifs and few people consider any of them too dry or too fruity. The taste is easily adjusted by adding soda and ice, and perhaps a slice of lemon.

Many red wines are too full and fruity to taste best by themselves; the finest reds are best with food. Those who like red wine above all others might like to try the following brands which are generally available, bearing in mind that a wine may vary from light and soft to fruity and dry, depending on the vintage.

---------------------------- *Light, Soft Reds* ----------------------------

These wines are generally light in fruit acids. One likes to take swallows of them instead of sips.

> AGE Rioja
> Rene Barbier Tinto
> Bodegas Bilbainas Vendimia Especial
> Castillo de Mudela Valdepenas*
> The Christian Brothers Claret
> Louis Martini Claret
> Bersano Barbera
> Borgogno Barbera

NOTE: Valpolicella and Bardolino can be quite dry, depending on producers.

---------------------------- *Light, Dry Reds* ----------------------------

These are wines that may taste sharp rather than watery or light in body. Their fruitiness inclines one to sip them rather than take several swallows.

> Undurraga Cabernet Reservado
> Concha y Toro Cabernet Sauvignon
> Premiat Cabernet Sauvignon
> Carmel Cabernet Sauvignon
> Adriatica Cabernet
> Cune Rioja Clarete
> Cambas Pendeli
> Achaia, Clauss Castel Danielis
> Bigi Chianti
> Louis Martini Zinfandel

NOTE: Zinfandel and most of the inexpensive California reds can be soft and light.

--- *Fruity Reds* ---

Some wines are easy to drink when young because their fruit acids give them a fresh, quenching quality. Beaujolais is the classic example, although many of those marketed today are full-bodied as well as fruity.

> Beaujolais-Villages
> Chinon & Champigny
> Bourgueil and Saint de Bourgueil Nicolas
> Côtes-du-Rhône
> Grignolino
> Chianti in Fiasco
> California Gamay and Gamay Beaujolais

--- *Full-Bodied Reds* ---

These wines are best sipped because they are full of taste from fruit acids and tannins. They are best when less than four years old, although some may need six years to lose their tartness, like Saint Emilions.

> Pinot Noir (Chile or California)
> Dão
> Rioja Reserva
> Saint Emilion Petits Châteaux
> Nebbiolo or Spanna
> Chianti Riservas
> California Petite Sirah

--- *...And the Best of All* ---

Dry Sherries—Fino or Manzanilla, which are chilled, and nutty Amontillado, which is not—are the best of all wines to serve before dinner. The British serve them at elevenses—a midmorning sipping, with biscuits or crackers—and serve Olorosos with cakes and cookies in the afternoon, before, after, or instead of, tea. Sometimes with.

Champagne and other sparkling wines are splendid before or in between meals; either Brut, or Extra Sec are preferred, Extra Sec perhaps with meals. People adore or abhor Champagne. Everybody likes the idea of it, though, the pop of corks, the feeling of jubilation.

Then there are the aperitifs based on wine: vermouths called French are dry, those called Italian are sweet (although dry and bitter vermouths are sold under the famous brand names), and there are the various brands like Dubonnet, Lillet, and Byrrh. These are served straight, on the rocks, with soda and a twist of lemon—any way you like. These aperitifs are preferred by those who want to reserve wines for meals and like something sharp or even sweet before sitting down to the table.

JUDGING WINES

A group of people confronted with a group of wines will rank them, picking winners. People tend to agree on the wines that are most drinkable. Precise rankings, however, are frequently meaningless. Wines that are being compared should come from the same grape, the same year, and the same region. Otherwise it is more of a sampling than a judging. Don't compare apples and oranges, says the trade.

Judges should be familiar with the wines, which should be limited in number, and there should be no effort to reach unanimity, declared wine authority Dr. Maynard Amerine, at a symposium conducted by the California Wine Institute. A judge making an awful face when he tastes may influence others to look for defects, he claimed; he called this tendency "stimulus error." Local judges may be sympathetic to wineries, erring on the side of leniency. Some judges may

> *Call for the best the house may bring,*
> *Sack, white, and claret, let them bring,*
> *And drink apace, while breath you have,*
> *You'll find but cold drink in the grave....*
>
> Beaumont and Fletcher
The Lover's Progress

stick to the middle range of scoring, which he called the "error of central tendency." "Time-order errors" occur when extraneous conditions like worry or noise impinge on judgments.

Dr. Amerine has some ideas about formal judging:

- Get a large number of responses so there can be some statistical measure.
- Maintain silence and physically separate judges.
- Code wines, hiding bottles and labels, presenting wines to judges in different orders.
- Have frequent rest periods if many wines are judged; but never judge wines after lunch.
- Judges should be familiar with the wines.
- Anchor scorecards by establishing break points and clearly define categories. 1-5 good, 6-8 very good, etc.

None of the above sounds like much fun. Informal judging can be, when the aim is to find wines that are a pleasure to drink rather than to find out what's wrong with them. Here are some ways to enjoy tasting a group of wines:

——————— *Ten Ways to Make Wine Tasting a Pleasure* ———————

1. Set up a buffet with some simple food—cold cuts, bread, cheese, a salad.

2. Select about six wines, preferably no more than ten, about which you are curious. The wines should be similar—from the same grape, year, and region—for most meaningful results. (This is called a *horizontal tasting;* a tasting of wines from the same vineyard or region but different years is called a *vertical tasting.*) If the wines vary widely in price, you can expect the costlier wines to be best— and you may be delighted to find bargains.

3. Mask the bottles so that the labels are hidden; set them out in a row and pour some wine in a glass in front of each bottle so that the color and smell can be judged. (Hiding labels is a *blind tasting;* in this way you discount judging based on name or fame, focusing attention on the wines. If you scrunch a paper bag around the bottle, that's called a *brown bag tasting.*)

4. When noting the wine in the row of glasses, ignore any that are cloudy or that look funny. Swirl each glass and smell the wine, pulling toward you those you like, pushing back those you don't. Taste first those wines you like.

5. Be optimistic. Wines that get in bottle are usually good. Try to find something to like in at least half of the wines, then try to define what you like about them.

6. Drink those you like with the food. Wine drunk by itself does not taste at all like wine drunk with food. A wine that tastes light by itself may taste better with bread and cold cuts or cheese than will a fuller wine.

7. Taste white wines well chilled. Taste those you like several times in the course of an hour.

8. Open red wines at least an hour before tasting them, pouring a glass as soon as the bottle is open. Taste those you like several times in the course of an hour, noting which taste better with cold cuts, which with cheese.

9. Talk about the wines only to those who want to discuss them, bearing in mind that the reason for the tasting is to find those you like. Sometimes it is fun to taste along with a companion, comparing notes, but most of the time comparisons are most interesting after judgments have been

made. (Do not scorn opinions of those who disagree with you, for they may simply be employing different standards of comparison.) Bear in mind that you will vary from day to day in your judgment, even from hour to hour, just as the wines vary. Enjoy any changes.

10. Buy a mixed case of three or more of the wines you like, or a case of each, drinking them at various times with various dishes. By so doing you explore the secret of wines, which is their variety.

———————TASTING SCORES———————

Wines are usually rated on a scale of 1 to 20, a couple of points for color, a couple for clarity, 4 points for aroma, and the rest for taste characteristics. Various positive impressions can be placed on a scale of intensity, from left to right, somewhat in the manner of those listed below. A vertical line connecting these points gives an impression of the wine at a glance. (Negative qualities are listed on the right.)

COLOR

White Wines:

watery	*silver*	*yellow*	*golden*	*colorless*
pale	*greenish*			*brownish*

Red Wines:

pale	*carmine*	*red*	*crimson*	*brownish*
rusty	*purplish*	*ruby*	*deep red*	*dull*

CLARITY

motes	*clear*	*bright*	*brilliant*	*cloudy*
particles				*dull*

SMELL

faint	*light*	*definite*	*pronounced*	*burnt, off*
	flowery	*fruity*	*complete*	*heavy*
absent	*pleasant*	*attractive*	*appealing*	

TASTE

Body (alcohol):				
watery	*light*	*pronounced*	*full*	*empty*
				heavy

Acidity:				
sharp	*fresh*	*tart*	*fruity*	*harsh*
light				*biting*

Tannin:				
bitter	*puckery*	*astringent*	*woody*	*rough*
bland				*rasping*

Maturity:				
green	*fresh*	*rounded*	*mature*	*empty*
raw	*lively*	*developed*	*complete*	*brackish*

Dryness:				
parching	*soft*	*dry*	*no sweetness*	*empty*
				flabby

Sweetness:				
fruity	*soft*	*ripe*	*honeyed*	*cloying*
flowery	*clean*			

NOTE: Any rating system should be personal. Instead of the suggested adjectives, you might choose a simpler way of considering the different elements of a wine, for instance:
> *Unacceptable; Okay, fair; Not bad; Good; Great Price.*

A close observer will note that the preceding ratings stress the importance of taste. However, experts agree that smell accounts for much of our judgment about wines. Should smell be scored as half, two-thirds, 90 percent?

An official German table has an interesting breakdown:

Color

Pale/oxidized	0
Light	1
Typical	2

Total not more than 2

Clarity

Cloudy	0
Clear	1
Bright	2

Total not more than 2

Smell

Off-smell	0
Expressionless	1
Clean and typical	2
Delicate	3
Well-developed/classic	4

Total not more than 4

Taste

Off-taste	0
Sound	1–3
Thin, weak, but clean	4–5
Pleasantly harmonious	6–9
Mature and elegant	10–12

Total not more than 12

The table looks as if it is arranged so that nobody loses, but note that a typical, bright, clean wine that is well-developed and pleasantly harmonious might only rank 14. To rate higher, a wine really has to have something, at least some elegance, some maturity.

Being clear, typical, and clean doesn't go far. But that's a passing grade. When there is nothing wrong with a wine, even though there is not much there, that's still really pretty good.

A good wine has wonder in it. A great wine is a marvel.

————MOST POPULAR IMPORTED WINES————

The following quartet amount to 80 percent of what's imported. You might like to sample them, well chilled with cold cuts, to see what America drinks:

Liebfraumilch: *Blue Nun, Hanns Christoff, Wedding Veil, and some 100 others. Sweetish white.*

Portuguese rosé: *Mateus, Lancer's, and a dozen others. Prickly pink.*

Sangria: *Yago, AGE, Siglo, and a score more. Sweetish red.*

Lambrusco: *Riunite, Calissano, Fabiano, and a score more. Fizzy red.*

NOTE: Prices range from $2 to $5. You might try sampling the higher priced wines in a single category, rather than tackling the group at once. Add ice, lemon, and soda for liveliness.

——————— TEN WINE SAMPLERS FOR TASTING ———————

Americans like to taste different wines to see what they are like. Here, for you to try, is a sampling of the wines we drink.

America gets more wine from abroad than any other country—and makes a larger variety on its own than anybody else—but very little of it is the "nice dry wine for dinner" that everybody claims to be seeking. Most of the wine sold is sweetish, and four bottles out of every five imported are somewhat meanly described as mawkish (see box). Few experts have ever done much more than let these wines graze their lips and you might fuddle them well by asking how many of them they have tasted lately.

─────────── *1. Flowery German Regionals* ───────────

The Rhineland sends us a gaggle of cheap regionals (the trade calls them inexpensive) that are certainly drinkable: not only Liebfraumilch, but those with brand names (and occasionally young wines ranked as Tafelwein, light but common) as well as others ranked higher as Qualitätswein or Qba, which is often fresh and flowery. Some of them bear township names, to which is added a fanciful name that might once have been a vineyard but now indicates a blend of lesser wines. Any three can be thirst-quenching when chilled, drunk either by themselves or with cold cuts:

    Brands: Deinhard Green Label. Fresh.

    Tafelwein: Moselblümchen. Light.

    QbA (Qualitätswein bestimmter Anbaugebeite or quality wine from delimited districts):

    Zeller Schwarze Katz. Often bland.

    Kröver Nacktarsch. Sometimes sharp.

    Bernkasteler Riesling. Sometimes fresh and light.

    Piesporter Goldtröpfchen. Often flowery.

    Johannisberger Riesling. Usually flowery.

    Niersteiner Domthal. Sometimes soft and flowery.

    Steinwein. Often fresh, light and dry.

NOTE: Brands and Tafelwein should cost well under $3. QbA wines that cost under $4 should have some freshness and floweriness, and you might choose to try a trio of these, perhaps with ice, soda, and a squeeze of lemon. Proprietary brands and Tafelwein can be disappointing; QbA wines can be as well, and they are not often exciting.

WHAT'S DRY IN EUROPE?

The Common Market has established standards for dryness, from 4 to 9 grams of sugar per liter. While other designations are not official, wines with less than 18 grams per liter can be considered medium dry. The following words may be considered more or less equivalent:

dry	*sec, secco, trocken*
semi-dry	*demi-sec, abboccato, halbtrocken*
medium sweet	*moelleux, amabile, lieblich*
sweet	*doux, dolce, süss*

——— 2. Italian Regionals: DOC, Superiore, Riserva ———

Half the wines we import come from Italy. What isn't from Lambrusco is mostly from the regions listed here. Most of these wines are dry, sometimes with a light sharpness, but generally fruity and fairly bland. The best regions come under control laws: DOC stands for *Denominazione di Origine Controllata;* slightly better grades are labeled *Superiore;* and wines labeled *Riserva* have to be at least three years old, and these are better.

NOTE: Wines under $3 are rarely worth buying; some of the Riservas can cost $6 and are worth it.

Try these with pasta or other Italian dishes, or with cold cuts or a barbecue:

> Chianti. Fruity and often nicely sharp; the best come in regular wine bottles, not in straw-covered fiaschi.
> Bardolino. A light red, generally fruity.
> Valpolicella. A fruity red, fuller than Bardolino.
> Soave. A soft and fruity white, nicely dry.

NOTE: A more interesting tasting would be to try all of the different Italian white wines you can find; have them with antipasto, pasta with clam sauce, and/or a veal or chicken dish, followed by cheese and fruit.

3. Portuguese Reds and Whites

Vinho Verde, meaning young wines, not green ones, comes from northern Portugal and is hard to find on the market. These are fresh and delicious, and low in price. You will be lucky to find more than one or two, so try also a Dão or Colares. When even these are not available, try some of the Spanish wines from around Barcelona: Panadés, Alella. Vinho Verde, which is pronounced VEEN-ho VARE-dzh, more or less, could become the most popular wines of the Eighties if importers begin bringing them in with regularity and in volume.

4. Alsatian Whites

A bewildering number of grapes are grown in Alsace, and the names are used on labels to identify the wines. While their prices are rising, the wines are worth exploring. Riesling is the most elegant, Gewürztraminer is the spiciest, Sylvaner the least regarded but full and soft. Tokay d'Alsace is made from the Pinot Gris and is fruity, balanced, often remarkable.

5. Mosel-Saar-Ruwer

This district produces the lightest, driest wines of Germany, perhaps the most pleasing and varied of any tasting of German wines. The least distinctive are blends from shippers labeled Moselblümchen, Krover Nacktarsch, and Zeller Schwarze Katz. Somewhat more pleasing are those from the main Grosslagen of the Mittel Mosel: Kurfürstlay, Michelsberg, Schwarzlay, and Münzlay. You may have to be satisfied with the Grosslage of the Saar, Scharzberg, or that of the Ruwer, Romerlay, but seek out any vineyard wines you can find. The vineyard wines of the Mittel Mosel may be expensive. The sampling will be sensational.

─────────────── *6. Europe East* ───────────────

From Austria to Romania, Hungary to Yugoslavia, delicious light wines are made that are lost on the shelves behind French, Italian, and California bottlings. Prices are as low as the demand, quality is often high. The wines are distinctive, not second best, and deserve to be drunk as casually here as they are in the home countries, especially with regional dishes. If the whites listed below are pleasing, you might choose to explore the reds.

Austria	Hungary	Romania	Yugoslavia
Grinzinger	Badacsonyi	Cotnari	Fruska Gora
Gumpoldskirchener	Somloi	Murfatlar	Ljutomer
Kremser	Balatonyi	Tîrnave	
Loibner		Odobesti	
Klosterneuburger		Cotesti	
Ruster		Panciu	

NOTE: The vines of the Rhine flourish along the Danube, and grape names usually follow the place names listed above. But look for wines of native grapes, like the Veltliner and Rotgipfler of Austria; Furmint, Hárzlevelü, and Keknyelü of Hungary; Feteascà and Creata of Romania; Kevedinka and Grk of Yugoslavia. French vines have been introduced. Two of the best Romanian wines are sweet, Cotnari and Murfatlar, to be tasted when found.

─────────────── *7. California Whites* ───────────────

The most popular sampling of California whites is always of the Chardonnay. Riesling samplings are most attractive if you like sweet wines. However, both would prove expensive. The most rewarding tasting would be of Sauvignon Blanc, **also** known as Fumé Blanc or Blanc Fumé; these are among the best California wines. The most varied tasting would be that of Chenin Blanc, also called Pineau de la Loire; the wines range from very dry to soft and fruity. Every winemaker is independent and adventurous, trying old and new methods in various combinations, so the variety of any wine is wide, and quality is high.

————————— 8. Bordeaux Whites —————————

People are forever tasting the red wines of Bordeaux—different districts, vintages from a single château, a collection of Petits Châteaux—but few have ever sampled many of the dry white Bordeaux. The least known are the new wines from Entre-Deux-Mers and the least tasted are Graves, now made drier than they used to be and among the best there are. Graves Supérieure is a rating reserved for white wines, and these are usually good buys. No better wines are made from the Sauvignon Blanc, except perhaps in California; quite different ones come from the Upper Loire, like Sancerre and Pouilly-Fumé. A selection of all these would be a fine sampling, with some sort of paté before a main course of fish or chicken, then cheese—white wines with all.

————————— 9. Rosés —————————

The waif among wines is about to become a Cinderella, transformed by winemakers around the world. Too many of the popular rosés have been sweetish and bland. There has always been Tavel and Lirac from the lower Loire, however, as well as the rosé de Cabernet of the Loire. Also, from California come some of the pale wines called whites but often rosy or faintly amber, made from red wine grapes. Rosé can be young and fresh, like those of Provence. When they are fruity but not sweet, they can become popular. Perhaps they will be the rage of the Eighties.

---------------------- *10. Reds* ----------------------

Red wines are often sampled because they are the wines most easily available. But red wines taste best—and different— with foods, and that is the way they can be most enjoyed. White wines are light enough to be drunk pleasurably by themselves, for the most part. During a meal, a party of four can sample six bottles or so.

Two or three red wines per meal is about all most people would care to try. A tasting of red wines is quite a different matter; as many as a dozen can be tried, then two or three served with buffet or a dinner, with the rest recorked and set aside for later.

A good tasting would concentrate on wines from the smallest of areas, and all of the same vintage—1976 Volnays, for instance—or a range of vintages from a single vineyard.

-------- *TEN CLASSIC WINE AND FOOD AFFINITIES* --------

"Red with fur or feathers, white with scales or shells or claws," goes the unappetizing old saw, with no hint at all of possible wonders. Red wines are delicious with chicken or veal or pork, but so are white wines. Turkey and stuffing are good with both, but any dry wine tastes terrible after cranberry sauce or candied yams; serve a slightly sweet wine here. A sip of dry wine should be followed by a taste of something sweet.

Salads, or anything with vinegar; all vegetables, especially spinach, asparagus, and artichoke; chocolate and ginger, spices like clove and cinnamon—all are supposed to be enemies of wine. But there are salad wines, particularly when the salad is more than greenery; examples are Chenin Blanc, Sylvaner, Beaujolais, Bardolino, any light wine that is flowery or fruity. Such wines are also good with cold cuts, antipasto, delicatessen, sandwiches. And vegetables with cheese sauces, eggplant, stuffed peppers, and squashes all taste better with the salad wines. Try a chocolate soufflé or mousse with Sauternes, gingery and spicy dishes with Rhine wines. One sip after a taste tells you if the wine is right. As for rosé, which is said to go with everything, it is best with things that are good with light red wines.

That still says nothing about wonder. Here are some classic combinations, marriages to make on earth, in which the wine makes the food sublime and the food makes the wine celestial—but try them and make your own hyperbole.

- *Caviar* Champagne, but also vodka
- *Foie gras* Sauternes
- *Oysters* Chablis
- *Clams* Montilla or Manzanilla Sherry
- *Trout* Moselle
- *Salmon* Meursault, but try Cortons or Montrachets, and especially California Chardonnays
- *Lobster or crab* Rhine Spätlesen, but see salmon, above
- *Ham* Vouvray, but also Riesling Kabinett, Gewürztraminer
- *Veal* Valtellina, but also Barbaresco, Gattinara, California Cabernet
- *Lamb, rack or leg* Bordeaux—Graves or Médoc Cru Classé
- *Roast beef or steak* Burgundy—Premier Cru or Grand Cru—but also Saint Emilion or Pomerol
- *Chicken, pheasant* Volnay, but also other Côte de Beaune Premier Cru or Rhines
- *Duck, game* Chambertin, but also Côte de Nuits Premier Cru
- *Walnuts, melon* Port
- *Pears* Sauternes, with cheese; but also Rhine Auslesen
- *Pastry, soufflé* Sauternes, but also auslesen

————————VERMOUTH QUIZ————————

Name Five of the Ten Main Ingredients of Vermouth

Blossoms	Peels
Leaves	Herbs
Stems	Spices
Barks	Alcohol
Roots	Red or white wine

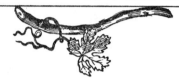

———————— LEADING WINE-DRINKING STATES ————————

It is not at all surprising that wines are drunk where they are made and where most people live. Nevertheless, quantities consumed spread over a wider range than would be expected. As the decade begins:

California is approaching consumption of 100 million gallons per year. New York consumption is nearing 50 million gallons per year. Illinois consumption is almost 25 million gallons per year. New Jersey and Florida drink close to 20 million gallons per year each. Massachusetts, Pennsylvania, Michigan, and Texas each consume some 15 million gallons each year. Washington state vineyard acreage is growing, but consumption was scarcely 12 million gallons a year in early 1980.

There are several states that consume some 8 million gallons per year: Connecticut, Wisconsin, and Oregon of the northern states; Colorado in the Rockies; Virginia, Maryland, and North Carolina along the Atlantic seaboard.

The southern trio is interesting when you consider that per capita consumption is highest of all in the District of Columbia, approaching 6 gallons per year. Congress and bureaucrats do not consume it all; prices are low in Washington and people drive from miles away to buy bargains.

Some states lead in per capita consumption because they are holiday centers that attract the convivial. Nevada consumption is only slightly less than the capitol's; that other gambling state, New Jersey, is expected to double its present consumption of about a bottle a month, or some 2½ gallons a year, by mid-decade.

New Hampshire ski country drinks close to 3½ gallons per capita annually; Vermont and Colorado are scarcely half a gallon less, as is seaside Rhode Island. Sunshine Hawaii, Arizona, and Florida approach 2½ gallons per capita a year.

If one considers adult population alone, the Pacific Northwest—Washington, Oregon, and Alaska—leads such populous states as New York, Massachusetts, and Connecticut. Consumption ranges between one and two bottles a month for those old enough to drink.

The states with lowest consumption are Kentucky and West Virginia, where those of drinking age manage scarcely a bottle per season. Iowa, Tennessee, Kansas, Arkansas, Mississippi, and Alabama drink something less than a bottle every two months. Oklahoma, Utah, North and South Dakota, Indiana, and Georgia may squeeze in an extra bottle or so for the holidays.

America is not much of a wine-drinking country, outside the cities and resorts. Californians of drinking age consume more than 30 bottles a year, which is not much compared with France, Italy, and Spain, where consumption is frequently reported to be about 30 gallons a year, or about a case of wine a month, for all.

Statistics are confusing, so individuals must rank themselves as to whether or not they are wine drinkers.

—————————— *QUIZ FOR WINE BIBBERS* ——————————

● *Do you drink wines only on special occasions like birthdays, holidays, and celebrations?*

There are perhaps a dozen such occasions in the course of a year. (Allow 3 glasses per celebration, or 36 glasses, averaging 3 ounces each. Figure 8 servings per bottle, which amount to 4½ bottles per year.) You could be from Kentucky.

● *Do you drink wines at least half the time when you go out to dinner in a restaurant?*

Many people go out to dinner once a month. (Allow 2 glasses of wine for an average of six dinners a year. At 3 ounces per glass, that equals 36 ounces or 1½ bottles. Add this to wine on special occasions, and total consumption comes to 6 bottles.) You may live in the South or on the Plains.

● *Do you drink wines when you go to friends for dinner?*

Many people average a dinner party at friends at least once a month, more in winter than in summer. (Allow 3 glasses of wine for each dinner party, which would be 9 ounces times 12, or 108 ounces, equal to nearly 5 bottles. Make it 6 bottles—who counts glasses at dinner parties? This brings your total to a case of wine, 12 bottles, a year.) You must live in a small city along a river, probably the Mississippi, the Ohio, or the Missouri.

● *Do you serve wines when friends come to dinner?*

Many people have a dinner party every month, but eight dinner parties a year is closer to the average. The number of guests ranges between four and six. (Allow a bottle of wine for each couple invited, omitting yourself to simplify figuring. Eight parties at two couples each equals 16 bottles. Add this to the 12 already counted, for a total of 28 bottles.) You must live in California or a big city.

● *Do you have an occasional glass of wine before dinner, even when there are no guests?*

A glass or two of white wine, with or without ice or

soda, is fashionable instead of highballs these days. People are also discovering the pleasures of Sherry and aperitifs, not to mention Champagne. Consider that perhaps once a week you might have a glass of wine or two with the family. (Allow 6 ounces of wine times 52 weeks, which amounts to 312 ounces or 13 bottles. Make it 12, because you might miss a week or two now and then. Add this to the previous 28 bottles, for a total of 40.) You probably live in Dallas, Los Angeles, Chicago, or even Boston.

- *Do you have a bottle of wine for dinner at home, even when only the family is present?*

Many people have wines with dinner, even when there are children at table. (Allow a bottle of wine for one such dinner a month, adding 12 more to your total. This brings you to a bottle of wine a week.) You probably live in New York, San Francisco, or Washington, or maybe you have a country place.

- *Do you occasionally have a big party with a buffet, and anywhere from 12 to 40 people?*

Most people have a party every season, if only to pay off social obligations. (Allow for four parties a year, the number of guests averaging 20. Allow a bottle of wine for each couple, or ten couples times four parties, or 40 bottles. Your yearly total is now 92 bottles. Add 4 bottles to round out the figures, and you have now consumed 8 cases of wine.) You probably have a European background.

- *Do you occasionally invite people for lunch, or for the afternoon, or perhaps for a quiet evening?*

Many people entertain casually once a month, over drinks. The number is usually 6 or 8. (Allow 1 bottle of wine for each occasion, considering that many people still drink cocktails and highballs. If you customarily serve lunch or snacks, make it 2 bottles. This brings your yearly total to 9 or 10 cases.) You live in a big city and have a nice group of friends, many of them European.

- *Do you keep white wines on ice for times when people drop in? Do you keep sparkling wine on ice? Champagne?*

People are always dropping in. Wines are now the fashion. (Allow for drop-ins every other week, one bottle per drop-in, or 26 bottles. Make it 24. You now consume nearly a case of wine a month.) You could be living in Paris, London, Rome.

—— *AOC, DOC AND VDQS—NOT TO MENTION QbA:* ——

Certain abbreviations help lead you to the best wines. How many of them can you identify correctly? 10 points for each answer.

> 50 or better—a wine lover, or amateur
> 60—an enthusiast, or frequent drinker
> 70—an expert, or constant reader
> 80—your average wine buff, or pedant
> 90—a connoisseur, or member of the trade
> 100—a vineast, or Rabelaisian, or Falstaffian

With the coming of the Common Market, leading wine countries—France, Germany, Italy—coordinated their control laws. They patterned them after French regulations that limited areas to be covered by place names, they ranked wines, and they specified how wines should be made. The French laws were developed by INAO, Institut National des Appellations d'Origine des Vins et Eaux-de-Vie, and the phrase used on bottles to identify the best wines is "Appellation Contrôlée." Similar simple letters and phrases now identify the Common Market wines. Can you explain the following?

France
● *AOC* Appellations d'Origine Contrôlées, which cover the top 20 percent of French wines. The phrase "Appellation Contrôlée" appears on every bottle marketed under such standards.

● *VDQS* Vins Délimités de Qualité Supérieure, which cover more than 50 wines, a second ranking of better-than-average wines that warrant protection of their names, vine-yards, vines from which the wines are made, and methods of tending and vinification. A stamp bearing VDQS appears on each label, with the phrase, "Label de Garantie."

●*VP* Vins du Pays, a third ranking of wines meant for current consumption and not exportation. The wines usually bear the name of the department where they are produced. They cannot be blended with wines produced elsewhere and must meet various requirements as to grape variety and vinification. *Note: Vins du pays* simply means wines of the countryside and has no official meaning.

●*Wine by percent alcohol* The lowest level of wines marketed in France simply carries on the label the amount of alcohol in the wine, as "Vin Rouge 11%," usually with a trademark or brand name to identify it. If the wine is French, the label will carry the phrase, "Produit de France," or even "Product of France." These rarely warrant the cost of shipping abroad.

Germany

●*QbA* Qualitätswein bestimmter Anbaugebiete, which means quality wine of designated regions, or regional wines that meet certain standards.

●*Tafelwein* A lesser ranking, for blends from regions of large production, identifies ordinary wines not warranting export.

●*Qualitätswein mit Prädikat* Special attributes, identi-fies wines of highest quality.

●*AP Nummer* Amtliche Prufnummer, a registry number that appears on labels, indicating that a wine has been tasted and found worthy of its designation.

●*VQPRD* Vins de Qualité Produits dans des Régions Determinées is a Common Market designation for all of the above. As other countries join the Common Market it may begin to appear on their wines meant for export.

• *VDPV* Verband Deutscher Prädikatswein Versteigerer, or Association of German estate-bottlers, actually a small group of the best producers, concerned with maintaining quality. Their wine labels show an eagle with a bunch of grapes forming his breast, surrounded by the letters of the organization. The symbol is a sign of superior wine.

Italy

• *DOC* Denominazione di Origine Controllata is the equivalent of the French AOC; under this name, the grape and vinification of wines are protected and limited to specific areas. More than 150 wines come under these laws but only a score or so are exported, among the best Italy produces.

• *DOCG* Denominazione di Origine Controllata e Garantita covers a few wines that are controlled and also guaranteed to come under even higher standards than DOC wines—usually a matter of limiting production and requiring higher percentages of alcohol and longer aging. The first of these were from the 1978 vintage and included Barolo, Barbaresco, Brunello, and Vin Nobile di Montepulciano, with Picolit and others to follow.

• *DOS* Denominazione di Origine Semplice or current wines that bear a geographic designation and follow local customs as to grapes and vinification. These rarely warrant exportation.

• *VSOP* Very Superior Old Pale, a phrase used to identify Cognacs of the best quality. The phrase has no official rating but is usually the best and oldest Cognac in the firm's line, containing brandies that may have been twenty years in cask. Cognac so designated can be the best buys of all, because the taxes for Three Star Cognacs and all other brandies are the same as for VSOP.

• *XO* Extra Old is a denomination used by some houses for old Cognac blends. Firms use various combinations of letters to indicate the various qualities they offer. One of these is the word "Napoleon," which has no meaning at all; the legend is that such Cognacs went to Moscow with Napoleon. Even if that were true, none of that is left in the marketplace. Thus the word signifies no more than a blend of Cognacs, indifferent or good, depending on the firm.

—— *QUESTIONS MOST OFTEN ASKED ABOUT WINE* ——

Many people find it hard to believe that wines are wonderful, infinitely variable, and worth the time, attention, and money spent on them. Doubts are best allayed by letting wines answer the questions. The truth is in the testing.

•*Do wines improve in the bottle?*

Buy wines of one of the Petits Châteaux of Bordeaux (see list on page 56), in several recent vintages, say 1978, 1976, 1975, 1973. Three vintages should be the minimum. Let them rest for at least a week after they have been brought home; stand them up a day before you want to taste them, open them an hour before you want to drink them. Serve them with cold cuts, cheese, or a simple dinner, starting with the youngest. The most recent wine is apt to taste bitter, a quality that diminishes as the wines get older.

Try the same with white wines to taste for yourself how wines can develop in the bottle.

•*What is roughness or harshness in a wine?*

A rough wine tastes sharp on the back of the throat, a quality not unpleasant in a young red that is full of fruit. The next time you are serving spaghetti or a stew, try a few rough reds to see how you like them.

Try to find a wine from Algeria or Argentina, tasting this against an inexpensive Rioja, a regional Saint Emilion, and a low-priced Cabernet from California. The harshest wines I know are those made from concentrate and sold in Canada; none of these is imported, though, and a trip to

Toronto is not worth the effort. Mass-produced California Cabernets are rough enough.

Note at the same time that some of the harshness is hidden under sweetness. Unless you pay attention, you scarcely notice the harshness, which is masked by the sugar.

● *How can you tell whether a wine is light in body or full?*

Body is a word used to describe the wateriness of a wine, and lightness can be a virtue, as can fullness. Taste the differences with German wines, chilling them well, then drinking them by themselves or with cold cuts.

The lightest German wines come from the Mosel-Saar-Ruwer region. Those of the Saar have been called "glorious water." Taste one of these against a Mosel, then against wines from the other districts, such as the light wines of Nahe or the much fuller ones from the Rheingau, or those that seem to have a certain heaviness from the Rheinhessen or the Rheinpfalz.

Or taste a Bardolino against a Valpolicella, then against a Chianti.

You might taste a couple of Beaujolais reds of different grades against the reds of the neighboring Chalonnais, Givry, or Mercurey. More strikingly, taste a range of Zinfandels from the different North Coast districts, one price level against another.

● *Why do you chill white wines and serve red wines at room temperature?*

White wines taste best when cold, young reds taste best when cool, reds two or more years in bottle taste best when at room temperature. Room temperature should be 70°F or less, about 20° Celsius. Wines taste cool when they are less than 60°F, and cold when they are 50°F or about 10° Celsius, which is cellar temperature. (The earth temperature stays between 50° and 55° year round and is perfect for keeping wines.)

An hour in a refrigerator cools a wine to 40° or so,

which is fine for Champagne and sweet white wines. Dry whites and young reds can be allowed to warm in the glass after an hour's chilling.

To see how coolness changes the taste of wines, chill a red and a white for an hour, then drink them with some cold cuts. The white will taste better at first, the red will taste better when it warms up. Cold numbs red wines, hiding complexities. Taste a Beaujolais against a Mâcon Blanc, or a Valpolicella against a Soave.

Don't chill expensive reds.

● *Does letting a wine breathe make any difference?*

Not to wines less than a year old or over twenty; such wines are poured directly into the glass and sniffed. The young wines may need five minutes or so to rid themselves of off odors, the old ones may be so far gone that they will turn to vinegar in a few minutes.

Almost all bottled wines improve with exposure to air. Many a wine opened when people sit down at table is fully developed when there are only a few sips left. Especially in restaurants, wines are drunk before they have opened up because the bottle was not opened soon enough.

Taste for yourself the next time there are six people or more for dinner. Plan to serve three bottles of the same wine, opening the first at least two hours before sitting down at table, the second an hour before, and the third as people are seated. Pour the wines one after another (everybody will need three glasses). The one that tastes best is sure to be the one first opened.

You don't let a wine breathe simply by pulling the cork. Pour off an inch or so into a glass so the air can get at it, as well as at the wine in the bottle.

———————— *WINES FOR EVERY DAY* ————————

Here are some wines to match the personality or change it.
Monday's child is fair of face
Sylvaner, Blanc de Blancs, Côtes-du-Rhône
Tuesday's child is full of grace
Meursault, Sauvignon Blanc, Volnay
Wednesday's child is full of woe
Graves Blanc, Champagne, Zinfandel
Thursday's child has far to go
Montrachet, Riesling Kabinett, Bordeaux Médoc Châteaux
Friday's child is loving and giving
Vouvray, Soave, Hermitage
Saturday's child works hard for a living
Chablis, Moselle, California Pinot Noir
And the child that is born on the Sabbath day
is bonny and blithe and good and gay.
Sparkling wines, Pinot Grigio, Beaujolais Crus

———————— *THE HUNDRED DAYS OF WINTER* ————————

Wines long in bottle change when the sap rises in the vine, when the vine flowers, during the vintage, and while the wine ferments. It is said that even if stored in darkness deep underground, where temperature and humidity are constant, the wine works. Or so goes the legend. Something beyond superstition, beyond practicality, urged the ancients to hold bacchanalia during the first days of winter when the new wines fell bright and during the last days of March in celebration of spring. No matter the reasons. Grand wines taste best in the winter.

Wine lovers insist that old wines in bottle go dumb during the vintage, even becoming cloudy in the fall and spring, losing bouquet, tasting off. In the summer, old wines don't taste right—maybe it's the heat—but young wines taste fine. After the leaves turn, before the daffodils bloom, that's the time for old bottles.

"You should have told me old wines are best in winter," accused a friend, disappointed with an ancient Burgundy saved for a June wedding. Wine dinners are held in winter, as are most auctions and tastings. You might stretch the hundred days back to October and up to April, spanning half the year. But there's no question about it: old wines taste best when frost is in the ground. Bacchus loves the hillsides, said Livy. The old pagan also loves the cold.

GLASSES

Many regions have developed their own glass shapes: for Bordeaux, almost that of a pear; for Burgundy, a big apple; for Rhine wines, a peach-like shape. The best glasses taper in at the rim and are filled less than halfway, so that the glass acts as a chimney to collect the bouquet of the wine. Glasses are usually stemmed so that the color can be seen easily when the glass is held. Wine buffs sometimes hold the glass by its base to get the best look at a wine held to the light, but this makes a glass hard to pick up or put down and may be considered pretentious.

Stemmed or not, wine glasses should be big, at least 12 ounces, so that the wine can be swirled without spilling. Swirling causes some of the alcohol to evaporate, bearing with it the volatile odors of the wine so that its bouquet can be smelled easily.

The best glasses are clear and crystal, with thin rims so that nothing detracts from the wine. Ornate glasses, etched, cut, or knobbed in various ways, make it difficult to see the wine; so does colored glass. Worst of all is the

Champagne coupe, said to be shaped after the breast of Helen of Troy, shallow and wide from rim to rim, easily sloshed. Regular wine glasses, tall and slim, are best for Champagne. Coupes are for sherbet.

———————— BOTTLE SHAPES AND COLORS ————————

Different wine regions have developed traditional shapes, but most wines are marketed in those similar to forms used in the three greatest wine regions. Burgundy bottles have sloping shoulders, Bordeaux bottles have high shoulders, and Rhine wines come in tall, slender bottles called flutes.

Brown glass is used for Rhine wines, green for Moselle and Alsace. Dark glass is used in Burgundy and Bordeaux as protection against light. Many light-colored bottles are used for wines meant to be drunk promptly. The best bottle color is considered to be dark brown, which is most resistant to light, but good wines are always stored in the dark so any dark color is adequate.

The bottom of the bottle is sometimes indented. This indentation is called the *punt*, sometimes the *push-up*. It is said to allow space for sediment to settle, but was probably devised so that bottles can be nestled together for storing, neck in punt. It is stylish to pour wine with the thumb in the punt, but this is awkward.

THE PRINCIPAL CHEMICAL CONSTITUENTS OF WINE
A dozen or so alcohols, mostly ethyl alcohol: 10–15%
Glycerol: 5–10gr/liter
A dozen or so organic acids, especially tartaric: 4–10 gr/liter
20 or so mineral ions, up to: 2 gr/liter
7 or 8 sugars, nonfermentable sugars less than: 2 gr/liter
* (up to 100 gr/liter in sweet wines)*
Gums and pectins (polysaccharides) up to:3 gr/liter
Phenolic compounds, some 50 substances:
* Red wines: 2–5 gr/liter*
* White wines, up to: 500 mgr/liter*
Nitrogenous substances, particularly proteins, numbering
* some 30, up to: 4 gr/liter*
A dozen or so vitamins
Some 150 odorous substances
…and water: 80%
Adapted from *Wine & Health*, edited by Salvatore P. Lucia, M.D.,
copyright 1969 by Wine Advisory Board.

--------- *BOTTLE SIZES* ---------

The familiar standard bottle is still called a *fifth*, from the fact that it was a fifth short of a quart, but wine bottles are now metric sizes. The standard wine bottle is 750 milliliters, or three-quarters of a liter, 25.4 ounces. A *magnum* or double bottle is 50.7 ounces or 1.5 liters. Wines mature more slowly in magnums, more quickly in half-bottles.

There can be confusion, for many ordinary wines are marketed in liter bottles of 33.8 ounces, and the difference in size is not readily noticeable. Bottles containing 3 liters, 101 ounces, are also marketed. Half-gallon bottles of 64 ounces can be confused with two-liter bottles of 67.4 ounces, both of which are disappearing from the market.

The French formerly produced a range of big bottles for the sheer pleasure of pouring them. A few are still produced to lend excitement to a party, most of them for Champagne. The bottles were given the name of Biblical kings and prophets.

Jeroboam	*Equal to 4 bottles*
Rehoboam	*6 bottles*
Methusalum	*8 bottles*
Salmanazar	*12 bottles*
Balthazar	*16 bottles*
Nebuchadnezzar	*20 bottles*

5.
Wine Buff's Alphabet: French, German, Italian, Spanish

---------------- FRENCH FOR WINE BUFFS ----------------
AN ALPHABET QUIZ

Eskimos have a hundred words for snow, it is said, and the
French have thousands for wine, wrenched from original
meanings, or coined, or adapted. Many of them are not
translatable and sound precious when the rounded, full-
mouthed French sounds are spoken in tight-lipped English.
Meanings are precise and often subtle and need to be experi-
enced, literally tasted or smelled, to be understood. Explanations are sometimes hilarious but are more often long-
winded. Casual wine drinkers can enjoy making up their own
words for tastes and smells.

    Bouquet, for example, refers precisely to the collection
of flowery and fruity smells that come from the alcohols and
acids in a wine. *Original bouquet* (the words are reversed in

French and the *g* is hard) is the smell of a wine before it is bottled. *Acquired bouquet (bouquet acquit)* is the smell of the wine after it has further developed in bottle, when the constituents have broken down and united. *Aroma* refers to the first smell of a new wine. And wine tasters call the bouquet the nose, as "The wine has a big nose."

The following terms are often misunderstood. How many can you correctly define? Score 5 points for each accurate answer, 3 points for answers essentially right, decision resting with the scorer. A score of 50 points is Excellent. Wine buffs might achieve 100 points.

● *Aligoté* Fruitful, second-rate grape of southern Burgundy, where it yields a quickly ready, quickly gone, refreshing wine—about a million gallons a year. Drunk as *vin de carafe* and usually used as a base for Kir, which is the Burgundian drink made by adding a dollop of currant liqueur, *créme de Cassis*, to a glass of the wine. Better versions are made with various white Burgundies, even those that are sparkling.

● *Appellation Contrôlée* Laws originated by winemakers, then made official, which control vine tending, yield, winemaking, and vineyard rankings of the top 20 percent of French wines. Nearly all the wines exported come under AC regulations. Sometimes called *AOC*, for *Appellation d'Origine Contrôlée*, the body of law.

● *Apéritif* The drink, often wine, served before a meal to whet appetite. These are usually sweet and flavored with various barks and herbs added to wine. Popular brands include Dubonnet, Byrrh, Lillet. Alcohol is added to bring them close to 20 percent. Not all are sweet—French Vermouth is not, for example—and the best are from Marseilles (Noilly Prat) or the Savoie (Chambéry).

● *Apre* French word for harsh, usually young wines bitter with tannin.

● *Arrière-gout* Aftertaste, lingering in a good wine, a diminishing continuation of the taste.

● *Balthazar* The biggest Champagne bottle being made, holding 16 ordinary bottles, occasionally produced for show.

● *Banyula* The most famous, and best, of *vins de liqueur*, sweet and lightly fortified, made in the Pyrénées foothills in the Côte de Vermeille.

● *Barrique* Word for a small barrel used in Bordeaux, equal to a Burgundy *pièce*, holding 225 liters or 24 cases of wine.

● *Cave* French word for cellar, often abused. *Mise en Bouteille dans nos caves* is often put on labels because it is close to official phrases meaning estate-bottling. All wines are bottled in cellars and the phrase is meaningless.

● *Cépage* Variety of vine and the grape from it.

● *Côte, Côteaux* Literally, side, meaning the slope of a hill, the best situation for vines, often used as the name for a wine district.

● *Crémant* Creaming, or fizzing. More than *pétillant*, less than *mousseux*.

● *Dame Jeanne* Large wine bottles held in wooden racks or wicker baskets, the original of demijohn.

● *Demi-sec* Literally half-dry, but actually referring to sweet wines.

● *Domaine* A vineyard, but it can also refer to a group of vineyards belonging to a single owner. *Mise du Domaine* or *Mise au Domaine*, or a variant, signifies wine bottled by the owner, an estate-bottling.

● *Dur* Literally, hard. A term hard to define, but referring to wine that is sharply acid or green, without any softness. This quality, which disappears with age, is sometimes characteristic of wines too young to be drunk with pleasure.

● *Egrappage* Destemming of grapes, done in an *égrapilloir*.

● *Elégant* Term meaning wines that show breed or have finesse, usually well balanced, often light.

● *Flute* A long, stemmed Champagne glass shaped like a thin V. Also the slim bottles used in Alsace.

● *Frais* Word meaning fresh, but also cool. *Servir frais* is to serve chilled.

● *Frontignan* Town where the best Muscat is made, the greatest *vin doux naturel*. Also a grape variety.

● *Gay Lussac* Man who devised a way of measuring alcohol by volume.

● *Grand vin* French for great wine, with no real meaning of any sort.

● *Grêle* Hail, the dread of wine growers.

● *Haut* High, or upstream, not an indication of quality.

● *Hectare* Metric equivalent of 2.47 acres.

● *Hecto* Short for hectoliter, 100 liters or 26.4 gallons or 11 cases of wine. Good vineyards yield somewhere between 30 and 35 hectos of wine per hectare in a good year.

● *Litre* A liter, about a quart or 33.8 ounces. The standard wine bottle is now 750 milliliters or 25.4 ounces.

● *Mâché* Chewy. Said of a wine that is full, one that fills the mouth and can almost be chewed.

● *Maderizé* Said of a wine that has taken on a brackish, strawlike taste and become brownish in color, from oxidation. The wine is considered to take on the taste of Madeira. In Madeira it is desirable, but not in white wines that are supposed to taste clean.

● *Millésime* The vintage year or date on a bottle.

● *Moelleux* Literally, marrowy or nutty, without sharpness.

● *Montrachet* The greatest of dry white wines, from Burgundy. Often mispronounced because the letters *t* are not sounded. Roughly, *mawn-rah-shay.*

● *Mousseux* Foamy, or fully sparkling, like Champagne.

● *Nature* Literally, a natural wine. *Champagne Nature* is one that has not been sweetened. Formerly Nature meant a still wine from Champagne, but the official phrase for that is now Côteaux Champenois.

● *Négociant* French word for a wine shipper. a Négociant-éleveur is a shipper who buys new wine and matures it.

● *Nouveau* New wine that has just been made, generally a wine less than a year old.

● *Oeil de perdrix* A wine that has the color of a partridge eye, somewhat bronze.

● *Pétillant* Lightly sparkling or crackling, a wine that has less than two atmospheres of pressure.

● *Pinard* Soldier slang for cheap red wine.

● *Primeur* First or springlike. The phrase *en primeur* applied to Beaujolais refers to the quickly fermented wine that arrives in Paris on November 15.

● *Race* Said of a wine that has breeding or elegance, often used in the past tense; a *vin racé* is well-bred.

● *Récolte* The crop or vintage.

● *Robe* Deep, clear color of a red wine, notably in Chambertins of Burgundy.

● *Sec* Dry. In a wine this is the opposite of sweet.

● *Seché* Dried out. Said of a wine that has lost fruit and freshness from having been stored too long in cask.

● *Sève* Sap or sappiness. Said of a wine that is not watery.

● *Tastevin* Knobbed silver saucer still used in Burgundy for tasting wines from cask. The *Confrerie du Tastevin* is the Burgundian promotion organization that swears in members as Chevaliers with much good-natured solemnity.

● *Terroir* The soil. A wine that has a *goût de terroir* has an earth taste, not unpleasant when light, rarely present in great wines.

● *Tête de cuvée* Literally head vat or first vat, an informal term for the best wine of a commune or firm.

● *Tranche* A word meaning a slice, applied in Bordeaux to a portion of a vintage, for which approved buyers are allowed to bid. Only those who have previously bought the wines of a châteaux are allowed to bid for the Première Tranche, or base bid, making purchase difficult for newcomers.

● *Tuilé* Wine that is the color of tile, tinged with orange, a sign that the wine is getting old.

● *Velouté* A wine with a texture of velvet in the mouth, somewhat more pronounced than a wine that is *soyeux*, or silky.

● *Vendange* The picking of the grapes, or harvest.

● *Verjus* The green juice of unripe grapes.

● *Vignoble* A nice contraction meaning vineyard expanse, of a particular area. In Burgundy, a vineyard is also called a *climat*, suggesting characteristics beyond soil and slope, including drainage and weather.

● *Vin Bourru* Onomatopoetic term for young wine, not completely fermented, that causes one to blubber one's lips after swallowing a mouthful, not always unpleasantly.

● *Vin cuit* Said of a wine that tastes cooked, from being made with concentrate or being heated to reduce volume and increase alcohol. Exceedingly unpleasant.

● *Viticulteur* A vine grower, not necessarily the owner of a vineyard but one who tends it and shares in the crop.

GERMAN FOR WINE BUFFS
AN ALPHABET QUIZ

So many of our words have Teutonic origins that we think we almost know what many of them mean, but those for wines get twisted. Mild, for instance, seems straightfoward enough, but when a Rhinelander says *meeld* he means a wine is not only gentle but also flowery and light and certainly beguiling. On the other hand, he may mean that the wine is simply low in alcohol. Tone has a lot to do with it; you have to taste the wine to get the word.

Then there is the matter of running words together, and of identifying a wine by the town it comes from, the vineyard, and the degree of sweetness. As a result we have what is said to be the longest name on the smallest label in the whole world: Eitelsbacher Karthäuser Hofberger Trockenbeerenauslese.

Because of the Germanic emphasis on precision, anybody taking the following quiz should get answers exactly right. Allow 5 points for each. A score of 50 indicates that you know your Liebfraumilch, 60 proves that you know the difference between a Zeller Schwarze Katz and a Bernkasteler, 70 that you can tell a Bereich from a Grosslage, 80 that you know a Winzergenossenschaft when you see one. A score of 90 means that you have been to the Mosel or should go. Anybody getting 100 is a Feinschmecker and should serve drinks all around.

●*Amtliche Prufnummer* Number on labels of the office bureau that checks German wines. The first number is the regional office that tastes the wine, the next three give vineyard location, the fifth through the eighth identify the bottler, the last two digits the year the wine was tasted. Its existence, more than the details, indicate the wine has been checked.

●*Anbaugebiet* Long for *Gebiet*, or region. There are eleven, but this word itself on the label is scarcely more than a regional identification of the wine. Quality ratings—QbA, Kabinett, and so on—are more meaningful.

●*Aus Eigenem Lasegut* The phrase for estate-bottling.

●*Auslese* Quality identification of wines attacked by the noble rot, made from selected bunches. Fruity and usually sweeter than Spätlese, which is made from late-picked grapes.

●*Beerenauslese* A wine from selected grapes, sweeter than Auslese, very expensive.

●*Bereich* Area in Germany, really a district within a region. For example, Bereich Johannisberg is a regional wine that can be made from any wines of the Rheingau; it's similar to one that is called Beaujolais or Côte de Beaune.

●*Bingen* Important township of the Rheinhessen, known for Scharlachberg, from a dark red hill behind the town, and for "Bingen pencils," German slang for corkscrews.

●*Bischofliches Konvikt* Also *Bischofliches Priester-seminar.* A refectory and seminary, respectively, that own important vineyards in the Mosel.

●*Bodenton* Earth taste, more frequently *Boden-geschmack.*

●*Brauneberg* Once called Dusemond and considered the greatest of Mosel wines, now less famous but still glorious.

●*Charlemagne* The great ruler of the Holy Roman Empire, responsible for establishment of many Rhineland and Burgundy vineyards. He was supposed to have seen a melted area where Schloss Johannisberger now stands and ordered that a vineyard be planted.

●*Creszenz* Growth. Like Wachstum. Either label formerly indicated estate-bottling.

●*Drachenblut* A belitting description of mediocre red wines.

●*Edelfaule* Noble rot, a fungus which splits grape skins, allowing water in the grape to evaporate, and thus permitting concentration of sweetness.

●*Einzellage* A single vineyard, as distinct from a Grosslage, which is made up of several small plots.

●*Eiswein* Wines of remarkable, rich sweetness, produced when grapes freeze on the vine and pressing leaves a concentrated juice.

●*Franken Riesling* Name for the Sylvaner that is planted widely in Franconia, and obviously an effort to cash in on the superiority of Riesling.

●*Gemeinde* A part of a district, a community, such as Bernkastel.

●*Grosslage* A misleading term: small vineyards were united during the Seventies into large ones, taking the name of a famous or important one that was absorbed. Not a vineyard wine, in the sense of a small area tended as a unit, but referring to a large vineyard with many owners.

●*Gutedel* German for the Chasselas or Fendant grape, making soft, ordinary wine.

●*Gutsverwaltung* A company that manages agricultural land, an estate-managing company.

●*Johannisberg* The town, the Schloss (castle), and the wines made at both. Also the general name for the Bereich of the Rheingau and the name in the United States for the noble Riesling.

●*Josephshofer* Superb vineyard in Graach, adjoining Wehlen, entirely owned by the Kesselstatt family. So great that only its name appears on the label.

●*Kabinett* The first grade of unsugared wines, Qualitätswein mit Prädikat, not always sweet, or even often, but fruity, flowery, and usually excellent.

●*Klevner* The Pinot Blanc grape in Germany and Alsace.

●*Kloster Eberbach* Great Rheingau monastery and estate developed by Cistercians (like Clos de Vougeot in Burgundy). Now stated owned, site of famous wine auctions and tasting seminars conducted by the German Wine Academy.

●*Lage* A vineyard. The best wines carry vineyard names.

●*Liebfraumilch* A blended wine, excellent when from leading shippers, usually sweetish, usually overpriced.

●*Mittel Mosel* The best section of Mosel vineyards, between Trier and Traben Trarbach.

●*Oechsle* Measure of sugar in the grape, a scale.

●*Ortsteil* Term for a vineyard so famous that its wines are sold with its name alone, like Burgundy Grands Crus.

●*Palatinate* The wine cellar of ancient Rome, today the Rheinpfalz.

●*Perlwein* Wines that are lightly sparkling.

●*Prädikatsekt* The best of German sparkling wines.

● *Prädikatwein* Those wines with special attributes, such as Kabinett.

● *QbA Qualitätswein bestimmter Anbaugebiete*, meaning Quality Wine of Specific Regions, sugared to bring them to minimum alcoholic standards, about 11 percent.

● *Qualitätswein mit Prädikat* Unsugared wines; Kabinett, etc.

● *Rheingau* Region producing the most distinctive Rieslings, full-bodied, balanced, and elegant.

● *Sankt Nikolaus Hospital* Charity hospital across the river from Bernkastel, owning some of the best Mittel Mosel vineyards, whose wines are sold at an auction similar to the one at the Hospices de Beaune.

● *Scharzhofberg* Most famous of Saar vineyards and one of the greatest; its wines are marketed with only the vineyard name.

● *Schaumwein* Sparkling wine in general, made in various ways, in bottle or bulk, with four atmospheres of pressure.

● *Schillerwein* Wine that shimmers, usually rosé, and ordinary.

● *Schloss* Castle. Three of them in the Rheingau are vineyards marketed simply with their own names: Schloss Johannisberg, Schloss Vollrads, and Schloss Reinhartshausen.

● *Schoppenwein* Slang for carafe wines or those sold in grocery stores.

● *Schwarze Katz* A blend of ordinary Mosel, a Grosslage of Zell.

● *Seeweine* Wines from the Bodensee, the north shore of Lake Constance, bordering Switzerland, of little export interest.

● *Sekt* The best of German sparkling wines, or Schaumwein.

● *Spätburgunder* German for Pinot Noir, few of which do well on the Rhine.

● *Spätlese* Wines from late-picked grapes, not always sweet, ranked just above Kabinett and below Auslese.

● *Spritz* Sparkle, usually light, like soda water.

● *Spritzer* The quenching German highball made of Rhein wine and soda water.

● *Steinwein* Originally from the vineyard of Würzburger Stein, then the name for wines of the whole region, which are now called Frankenwein, mostly Sylvaner and Müller-Thurgau.

● *Stück* Large German cask but often a measure of 1,200 liters, about 133 cases.

● *Süss Reserve* Sweet reserve, unfermented grape juice added to the wine for sweetness.

● *Tischwein* Table wine, but used derogatorily of carafe wines.

● *Traubensaft* Grape juice, the kind that's drunk.

● *Waldmeister* Woodruff, the herb used to spice May Wine by steeping for a few hours.

● *Weinbaugebiete* Wine-growing region.

● *Weingut* An estate, including vineyards, winery, and cellars.

● *Weingutbesitzer* One who sits on a Weingut, the owner.

● *Weinstrasse* Literally, a wine road, but especially the one through the vineyards of Rheinpfalz.

● *Weissherbst* Lovely name for a little wine from the Bodensee.

● *Winzer* Wine grower, usually one who works his own vineyard.

● *Winzergenossenschaft* A cooperative of wine growers, usually big.

● *Winzerverein* A local wine growers' association, usually small.

ITALIAN FOR WINE BUFFS
AN ALPHABET QUIZ

Wines listed below are little known, all are worth discovering. Score 5 points for recognition, however vague, 10 points if the wine has been tasted.

Ranking:
50 or better—wine lover, or amateur.
60—So you've tasted more than Chianti?
70—You must be Italian.
80—Try wines from elsewhere.
90 or better—Drink more, read less.

●*Amarone* Dry red wine from raisinized grapes that are further dried on racks, usually made in December or later. Best from Veneto or Piedmont, and especially Valpolicella Recioto, which is half-sweet like a light Port and, less fortunately, *frizzante* or somewhat fizzy.

●*Buttafuoco* Dry, light red of southern Lombardy, whose name means shooting fire; one of a trio with Barbacarla (Charlies' beard) and Sangre de Giuda (Judas blood) whose names are more striking than their tastes. On a par with Zeller Schwartze Katz or Kröver Nacktarsch.

●*Brunello* Dry, noble red, perhaps the longest-lived Italian wine, made from the grape of the same name, a version of San Giovese, in the town of Montalcino near Siena in Tuscany. Made famous by Biondi Santi, whose family still produces the best.

●*Cortese* Dry light white of the Piedmont, from the grape of the same name, which means courteous (as Soave means suave.). To be drunk young. The best is from Gavi.

●*Dolcetto* Soft red wine from the grape of the same name, from Alba. Dry, and best when young.

●*Etna* The best wines, red and white, of Sicily, grown high on the slopes of that somnolent volcano.

●*Freisa* Red wine grape of the Piedmont, producing fine dry reds that are elegant (and half-sweet or half sparkling wines, *amabile* or *frizzante*, that are not). Best is from Chieri.

●*Gattinara* One of the great Piedmont reds, ranking with Barbaresco and Barolo.

●*Governo* Practice of adding the ferment of raisinized grapes to Chianti that has already fermented, inducing a little

176

second fermentation that gives the wine a prickly feeling in the mouth.

● *Grignolino* Piedmont grape that makes a red wine that tastes light but isn't, for it can reach 14 percent alcohol.

● *Marsala* Usually sweet wine of Sicily devised by English expatriates to compete with Sherry and Port. Lightest is Italia Particolare, IP, with 5 percent sugar; Marsala superiori can be dry, or must have 10 percent sugar if sweet: Marsala vergini is always dry. Various aperitif wines are made by adding eggs, quinine, or other flavoring ingredients.

● *Montepulciano* The *vino nobile* of this Tuscan hill town was one of the first reds to be ranked DOCG *(Denominazione di Origine Controllata e Garantita).*

● *Picolit* Legendary dessert wine, but not too sweet, one of Italy's rarest and greatest, from Friuli.

● *Primativo* Red wine grape, planted in Italy's heel, that is used for blending and is the ancestor of California's Zinfandel. (A relation is Plavac from Yugoslavia.)

● *Pulcianello* Bottle used for Orvieto, this is a stubbier version of the straw-covered Chianti *fiasco.*

● *Santa Maddalena* Fruity, light red, one of the best from the Italian Tyrol, from Schiava grape.

● *Terlano* Tyrolese white; pale, soft, but dry.

● *Termeno* Tyrolese source for Gewürztraminer.

● *Valtellina* Great reds of Lombardy, from the Nebbiolo grape, full and long-lived from slopes of Sassella, Grumello, Inferno.

● *Vermentino* Best dry white of the Italian Riviera, pale and fresh.

● *Vernaccia Sardinian* Dry white, often intense, which can be 17 percent alcohol, perhaps the most potent natural wine made.

● *Vino da arrosto* The Italian for big wines best with roasts, like those of the Piedmont.

● *Zucco* Famous sweet Muscat of Sicily, perhaps surpassed by Moscato di Siracusa or the Sardinian Cagliari.

————————— *SPANISH FOR WINE BUFFS* —————————
AN ALPHABET QUIZ

The Spanish have a certain nonchalance about wine, so when taking the quiz the scoring should be easy: 10 points when the answer's fairly right, an extra 5 if the answer shows imagination. A score of 50 shows you know where Amontillado comes from, 60 that you are an aficionado of something Spanish, not necessarily wine, 70 that you like to watch flamenco or listen to guitars, depending. A score of 80 indicates you know that Rioja is a light wine and not a heavy one, 90 that other wines are better with paella than sangria. A score of 100 calls for a glass of Manzanilla.

●*Amontillado* A nutty, aged Sherry the color of hazelnuts, made in the style of the lighter, drier wine of Montilla. Marvelous with nuts, fruit cake, custard.
●*Cheribita* Spanish twisting of sherry-and-bitters, a startling morning drink invented by the English and occasionally offered in southern Spain.
●*Cosecha* The vintage year, indicating the harvest from which the majority of the wine has been made.
●*Espumoso* Spanish word for sparkling. Most of these wines are sweet—but try Cordoniu.
●*Fino* Dry, yeasty Sherry, best served chilled, with nuts, slivers of ham or cheese; superb with cold shrimp and other seafood, fish with mayonnaise.
●*Gran Riserva* Applied to the best grades of old Riojas, used almost interchangeably with Imperiale. Perhaps the driest of fine red wines.
●*Manchego* Wine from La Mancha, often ordinary, but taste the reds from the district of Valdepenas.
●*Manzanilla* Dry Sherry from the seacoast town of Sanlucar de Barrameda, with a parching, almost salty taste. The wine of bullfighters. It is perhaps the driest wine in the world.

●*Oloroso* Literally, fragrant. Intense quality in old wines, the type that is the basis for sweetened cream Sherries. A classic dessert wine, often chilled. Also frequently drunk by itself or with biscuits, wafers, or sweet cookies.

●*Penedes* District near Barcelona being replanted in noble vines; look for Pinot Noir.

●*Ribiera* Wines near the Portuguese border, like vinho verde.

●*Rueda* Good white wines from Old Castile.

●*Toro* Good red wines from district adjoining Rueda.

●*Valbuena* Reds from vineyards in the valley of the Duero, ranked with the best Riojas, and above them.

—ALCOHOL COMPARISON BY WEIGHT AND VOLUME—	
Grams per liter	*Percent by volume*
80	10.08
90	11.34
100	12.60
110	13.86

6.
Your Wine Horoscope and Other Lore

———————— *YOUR WINE HOROSCOPE* ————————

Dionysus, god of wine and vine, was the son of Zeus and Semele the earth goddess. His Roman incarnation was Bacchus, who presided over some of the best, or worst, of the ancient revels. The gods of wine have always celebrated the change of seasons—with the tasting of the new wine at the winter solstice; during the festival of joy at the spring solstice—and whenever there was need to banish care. Vintage festivals (when the vats were cleaned at the end of January, Midsummersnight Eve) and rites that involved other gods and goddesses all required wine. The first bacchanalia were attended only by women. When men were finally admitted, the revels became so wild that the rites were banned, although vestiges may still exist in southern Italy. And elsewhere.

181

Perhaps because of the ancient ban, wine lovers seem never to have been linked to the moon and stars and the mystic patterns set out through the centuries. Certainly there are wines for all seasons and all temperaments. Herewith, a consideration of which wines suit whom, and when, a task made uncertain by the widely held belief that any wine goes, anytime. Anybody happening on a bacchanalia today might take notes on possible discrepancies.

———————————— *Signs of Spring* ————————————

Aries • 21 March–19 April
The ram, cardinal sign of fire, ruled by Mars. Flaming red the color, blazing diamond the stone, Tuesday the lucky day, 7 and 8 the lucky numbers. Dominant is the head, domain is the desert.

Daring children of spring, exploring wild places, often reckless, apt to keep Beaujolais of a bad year to see how it will taste a decade hence, make a white wine of Zinfandel or sparkling Cabernet. Also likely to plant vineyards in odd places—Maine or Texas—and plant hybrids. Always first to try new wines like those from Washington or Russia, Oregon or Algeria, Ontario or Chile. Tendency to drink clarets too young and Meursault too old. Always searching for bargains among California and Spanish jug wines, discovering the white wines of northern Italy, the reds of Yugoslavia. Prefer lamb, goat cheeses, figs, and spicy dishes. Will try any wine twice, particularly if it is young and red.

Aries wines: Beaujolais Cru, Rioja Clarete, Zinfandel, Chenin Blanc or Blanc Fumé, Vinho Verde, Pinot Grigio.

Taurus • 20 April–20 May
The bull, fixed sign of earth, ruled by Venus. Green the color, emerald the stone, Friday the lucky day, 1 and 3 the lucky numbers. Dominant is the throat, domain is on the plain.

Forceful and vital, even stubborn, always willing to talk or shout praises, apt to insist that a wine is getting better even as it gets worse, that a wine is dry when it is half sweet, that one is clear when it is cloudy. Would make a successful restaurateur or wine salesman. Tendency to keep wines too long and pour them too slowly. Prefer heady wines of deep color, California Cabernet over claret, Auslese over Kabinett, Barolo over Chianti. Famous wines appeal rather than new, unknown wines, no matter how good. Once they are discovered, become passionate about dry Fino Sherries and Vintage Ports. Prefer beef, milk cheeses, olives, and thick stews. Drink old wines in preference to young.

Taurus wines: Rhônes (particularly Hermitage), Rheingauers, Napa Cabernets and Chardonnays, Piedmont Barolos, and Gattinaras.

Gemini ● 21 May–20 June

The twins, changing sign of air, ruled by Mercury. Blue to gray the colors, pearl the gem, Wednesday the lucky day, 3 and 6 the lucky numbers. Dominant the shoulders, domain the mountains.

Quickly generous, quickly changing, in a world of opposites, apt to choose Burgundy one moment, Bordeaux the next, a light Riesling now, a full Montrachet later—and much of any—and sometimes none at all for weeks. The moonstone, said to protect from drunkenness, is also the gem for the twins, presaging success as a wine steward or cellar-master. If a winemaker, shows a tendency to make two wines at once—a quickly vinified Chardonnay aged in oak, for instance, and a slow vinification soon bottled. Apt to essay strange dinner combinations—starting with a Sauternes and foie gras, as an example, followed by Beaujolais and hamburgers—and Champagne with the cheese. Prefers fowl of all sorts, goat cheeses, berries and sauced dishes. Likes any wine, at times.

Gemini wines: Dry white wines and fruity reds, especially Burgundies, and clarets, particularly Médocs. Also Graves and Canon-Fronsaca, Vinho Verde and Condrieu.

————————————— *Signs of Summer* —————————————

Cancer ● 21 June–22 July
The crab, cardinal sign of water, ruled by the moon. Silver the color, ruby the stone, Monday the lucky day, 3 and 8 the lucky numbers. Dominant is the chest, rivers and trees the domain.

Intuitive and creative, a thoughtful striker of balances between formal and casual, apt to serve Chambertin in Baccarat with steaks charred in the fireplace, or Champagne on picnics. Moon children make an easy art of wining and dining—when left alone. Fond of any good wine and excellent judge; like a good Beaujolais, a fine Burgundy or claret or Rhône, but not wines too fruity, too heady, too intense. Particularly abhor sweetish wines, although tolerant of Sauternes with a pear. Prefer wines that are subordinate to foods but that complement the dishes. Superior at suiting one thing to another. Prefer beef, strong cheese, melons, and well-seasoned, even hot, dishes. Will try any wine, but like only those well developed and balanced.

Cancer wines: Ten-year-old clarets, eight-year-old red Burgundies, five-year-old white Burgundies, Champagne.

Leo ● 23 July–22 August
The lion, fixed sign of fire, ruled by the sun. Gold the color, ruby the stone, Sunday the lucky day, 3 and 1 the lucky numbers. Dominant is the heart, castles the domain.

Vigorous wines of the south, gold and ruby, excite these bold summer people. The wines are changelings, but not their adherents, who like the soft and often sweetish wines with seafood and pork dishes, the reds with game and roasts. Apt to pour too much too often, not only for others, Leos are splendid innkeepers and better hosts, though extravagant. Choice of many wines is more desirable than a few choice bottlings. Prefer game, blue cheeses, peaches and pears, strongly seasoned dishes, preferably with garlic. All wines welcome.

Leo wines: Italian wines, California wines, Rhône wines, all with abandon.

Virgo ● *23 August–22 September*

The virgin, changing sign of earth, ruled by Mercury. Sapphire the color, sapphire the stone, Wednesday the lucky day, 8 and 5 the lucky numbers. Dominant is the head, home the domain.

Ordered and precise, taming confusion, with a tendency to serve rosé to resolve conflict, or beer to evade argument. Apt to select a wine in the middle of a list, neither the dearest nor cheapest. Avoid new wines and old ones, seek abundant vintages of average quality. Choose wines not too dry and not too sweet, not too full, not too light. Prefer Châteauneuf-du-Pape to Hermitage, Graves Supérieur to Blanc de Blancs, Mâcon Blanc to Pouilly-Fuissé. Like Chianti, Amontillado, Tawny Port, Soave, Anjou rosé, Saint Emilion. Put jugs of imported red and white on the buffet. Prefer chicken and seafood, runny cheeses, apples, and lightly seasoned dishes.

Virgo wines: Sparkling wines, Côtes-du-Rhône, Alsatian whites, Provence rosé.

--------- *Signs of Autumn* ---------

Libra ● *23 September–23 October*

The balance, cardinal sign of air, ruled by Venus. Sky blue and gold blending to green is the color, opal the stone, Friday the lucky day, 6 and 4 the lucky numbers. Dominant is the spine, domain the earth.

Hopeful, even idealistic, artists of the casual, apt to order the house wine with the speciality of the day, white wine and salad in a steak house, lobster and Champagne in a seafood restaurant. Buy wines on sale or those frequently advertised, and will try anything new on the market, serving them with omelets, casseroles, or stews. Prefer bottles with screw tops, jug wines of all sorts, imported wines over American bottlings. Prefer roasts to chops, cheeses that slice, fruits of the season, well-seasoned dishes.

Libra wines: Jug wines or those in magnums, reds from France or Spain, whites from Italy. Petits Châteaux from Bordeaux, Chianti, and Mâcon Rouge are favorites.

Scorpio ● 24 October–21 November
The scorpion, fixed sign of water, ruled by Mars. Red the color, topaz the stone, Tuesday the lucky day, 5 and 4 the numbers. Dominant are the genitals, domain the cave.

Moody and passionate, charming and shrewd, Scorpios like anything so long as it is excellent. Apt to buy Champagne (nonvintage) instead of sparkling wines, estate-bottled Burgandies and classified growths of Bordeaux instead of regionals. Seek good wines of the best vintages. Tendency to reject suggestions of the wine steward or the expert, choosing old wines over young ones—except for the best Beaujolais. Excellent judge of wines, with a tendency to scorn wines that are merely good. Abhor semisweet wines and those that are too light or too heavy, but will drink a single glass of a superior sweet wine with a ripe pear or soufflé. Prefer French wines above all others, but like Rioja. Prefer veal, goat cheeses, melons, and lightly sauced dishes.

Scorpio wines: Classed Growths of the Médoc, Graves and Pomerol, Côtes Canon Fronsac; California Chardonnay; Volnay, estate bottlings of Vosne-Romanée; Manzanilla Sherry; Vintage Port.

186

Sagittarius • 22 November–21 December
The archer changing sign of fire, ruled by Jupiter. Purple the color, turquoise the stone, Thursday the lucky day, 9 the number. Dominant are the thighs, quicksand the domain.

Understanding, restless, and independent, prefer Beaujolais of the best growths and young whites within a year of the vintage, Loires over Alsatians, Côte de Beaunes over Côte de Nuits, Gattinara over Barolo. Usually reject wine steward suggestions, except in the best restaurants. Ignore rare and famous wines in shops, particularly Pommard and Pouilly-Fuissé, the Grands Crus of Bordeaux, and Auslesen from the Rhine—but will drink them when offered. Prefer sparkling wines to Champagne because of price. Seek good wines of copious vintages, great wines in off years. Like the lesser dry wines of California, especially Chenin Blanc and Petite Sirah. Dislike sweet wines, and wines kept long in wood. Prefer veal and pork, goat cheeses, limes and lemons, dishes with thin sauces. Always try new wines.

Sagittarius wines: Estate-bottled Beaune and Corton; Meursault and Chassagne-Montrachet; Muscadet, Sancerre, and Chinon; Valpolicella and Pinot Grigio.

Signs of Winter

Capricorn • 22 December–19 January
The goat, cardinal sign of fire, ruled by Saturn. Black the color, garnet the stone, Saturday the lucky day, 7 and 8 the lucky numbers. Dominant are the knees, bastions the domain.

Dependable and patient, order red wines over white because there is more of it. Stick to well-known wines because there is less risk of getting a bad bottle. Buy lesser wines of great years and tend to keep them too long. Find a wine that is satisfactory and buy it again and again. Prefer Bordeaux to

Burgundy because they've had a world market longer. Distrust Italian, Spanish, and Portuguese wines because they vary so much, and think California is coming along but is too expensive for the best wines from the best grapes. Buy good wines of the highly rated vineyards. Prefer Pomerols to Saint Emilions because Merlot is a better grape than Cabernet Franc. Like Cahors because it is made from Malbec, Hermitage and Côte Rôtie because the vines are the true Syrah. Buy German wines of Kabinett grade and better, although preferring dry wines to sweet. Prefer beef, Roquefort, preserved fruits, and dishes without sauces. Buy any established brand.

Capricorn wines: Estate-bottlings and château-bottlings of the Rhine; Burgundy, Bordeaux, Cream Sherries, Vintage Port.

Aquarius● 20 January–18 February
The water bearer, fixed sign of air, ruled by Uranus. Blue the color, amethyst the stone, Saturday the lucky day, 1 and 3 the lucky numbers. Dominant the legs, caverns the domain.

Calm, but sometimes wild, apt to order Beaujolais because it does not have to breathe or be chilled and is at its best when cool from the cellar. Buy white wines because there is less fuss about them. Consider wine steward suggestions, but settle for Pommard, Pouilly-Fuissé, Chianti. Marked tendency to try red wines with seafood at times, just to see if they agree with expert opinion that prefers whites. Suspicious of vintage charts and official ratings—but check them before buying. Buy jugs for parties, preferably those labeled "Imported," never spend more than five dollars for a bottle—but get carried away at celebrations, convivialities, and when the moon is full. Buy middle-priced claret, making a rule to cellar it at least five years before drinking. Truly prefer white wines, with only an occasional Beaujolais or Chianti when guests insist. Like beef but eat fish and chicken to keep slim, prefer hard cheeses, apple, and plain food.

Aquarius wines: Rated clarets, town wines of the Côte

de Nuits, but mostly Graves whites, Loires, Rhines, Swiss and Austrian whites.

Pisces ● 19 February–20 March
The fishes, changing sign of water, ruled by Neptune. Sea green the color, aquamarine the gem, Tuesday the lucky day, 8 and 4 the lucky numbers. Dominant are the feet, domain the depths.

Loving, imaginative, always making something, apt to make a meal of the first course, drinking first white and then a light red, with a sweet wine for dessert. Prefer dry white wines from Montrachet to Muscadet, Asprino from Naples to Zwicker from Alsace, variety and plenty being as important as excellence. Notable tendency to mix drinks, especially to blend tart jug wines with bland ones, to add lemon, soda, and ice to improve the drink. Ignore fashionable wines, except when offered. Like to try rosé to see if it is dry enough, then order a curry or sauced fish dish when it is not. A superior taster and judge of wines, particularly of whites. Superb winemaker, and an excellent blender of wines, especially of Champagne cuvées, dry Sherries—and Scotch. Drink beer because it is there. Like all food, preferably from fine cooks, but prefer fish, veal, fowl, and seafood, goat cheeses, melons and limes, unusual dishes.

Pisces wines: White wines of all sorts, dry when possible, Manzanilla Sherries, Champagnes and sparkling wines, the sharp, dry whites of Switzerland such as Neuchatel and of New York state such as Aurore.

──────── *WINES FOR THE FULL OF THE MOON* ────────

	California	*France*	*Italy*
SPRING			
April/Seed moon	Zinfandel	Beaujolais	Bardolino
May/Hare's moon	Gewürz-traminer	Muscadet	Pinot Grigio
June/Dyad moon	Grenache Rose	Tavel rosé	Chianti
SUMMER			
July/Honey moon	Johannisberg Riesling	Sylvaner	Frascati
August/Wort moon	Chenin Blanc	Sancerre	Verdicchio
September/Barley moon	Sauvignon Blanc	Chablis	Cortese
FALL			
October/Blood moon	Chardonnay	Meursault	Soave
November/Snow moon	Gamay Noir	Beaujolais Nouveau	Valtellina
December/Oak moon	Sparkling Californian	Champagne	Asti Spumante
WINTER			
January/Wolf moon	Cabernet Sauvignon	Pomerol	Barolo
February/Storm moon	Pinot Noir	Volnay	Gattinara
March/Virgin moon	Petite Sirah	Hermitage	Valpolicella

──────── *THE SEVEN AGES OF A WINE DRINKER* ────────

● *The Quaffer* Drinks wine when beer is too sour, soda pop is too sweet, coffee is too hot, and tea is too weak—or when it is there.

●*The Faddist* Drinks white wine in place of cocktails and highballs because it is sophisticated, red wines with meals because everyone else does. Rosé is scorned because it is not smart, sweet wines because nobody else drinks them. Bubbles are stirred out of Champagne because that's what the international set does, preferably with swizzle sticks of silver or gold.

●*The Tyro* Discovers that there are more wines than Beaujolais, Chianti, and Soave, that all of them taste good with food, and that they add pleasure to the company.

●*The Amateur* Likes more than Chardonnay from Burgundy and California, seeks out Cabernets from everywhere, and wants to taste everything new on the market. Hankers after a Fino or Manzanilla before dinner, Ruby or Tawny Porto after dinner, and Champagne whenever a cork pops.

●*The Buff* Not only drinks wines in preference to everything else, but reads about them, talks about them, holds and goes to tastings and auctions, will travel out of the way to visit vineyard or cellar and go across the town, the continent, or the sea for a wine dinner. Drinks reds (when more than four years old) only in the Hundred Days of winter. Enthusiasm overcomes occasional lapses into verboseness, pedantry, exaltation. (Not to be confused with the wine snob; see note below.)

●*The Connoisseur* Drinks wine even with a sandwich, will skip a course to be able to afford a better bottle, spends too much time arranging dinners for great bottles, selects guests for their awareness rather than their charm. Prefers simple dishes that show off the wine, expresses opinions in few words in a low voice, hides feelings when a wine is poor or badly served. Sends dishes back in restaurants—and bottles—and tips frugally. Buys by the case when wines first appear on the market. Knows every good cellar within a hundred miles.

●*The Wine Lover* Considers the winemaker the greatest of artists, talks wine with buffs and connoisseurs, encourages tyros and listens to others about wines, usually responding with *ah ha, uh huh,* or *um.* Avoids negative comment of all sorts, finding what's good in a wine, not its flaws, leaving poor wines tasted but undrunk. Interested in others' comments about wine and their enjoyments. Takes all wine as it comes, is a good host or hostess, matching bottles to the company and the food. Has a small cellar of good wines, with which he is lavish.

NOTE: There are other categories of wine drinkers, among them THE WINE SNOB, *usually an old faddist who has not outgrown social pressures or the inexperience of ignorance. The Snob drinks only famous wines from vintages identified as great, preferring the expensive to the reasonable, the label to the wine. Talk largely focused on cost, on names, on adjectives. Really prefers whiskey—or vodka, preferably imported. Has some knowledge that is constantly displayed, however inaccurate or prejudiced.*

———————————— SUPERSTITIONS ————————————

Wine is mystery, a thing of wonder, and while St. Paul tried to make common sense of it by calling it a good, familiar creature, the lore is filled with superstition. Wine brightens the disposition marvelously, a gift of the gods, according to the ancients. Going against custom can bring bad luck, which can easily be avoided by doing things properly; not to do so is today considered gauche, or even bad manners.

Not so long ago women were not allowed in wine cellars, and grandfathers still get uneasy at their presence near the casks, believing they might sour the wine. In spite of Hebe, cup bearer to the gods, the ritual of opening a bottle and pouring the wine is the task of the host. Wine is poured first in the host's glass, to assure his guests that it has not been poisoned. Porto is poured only after the women have retired from the dining room; guests fill their own glasses, passing the bottle clockwise around the table. Nobody knows why. In the Champagne country, corks are not allowed to pop. In Jerez, you never have a final glass of Sherry, but always the next-to-the-last glass, *la penúltima copa*.

Honoring custom is a sign of sophistication—certainly, there is nothing superstitious about it—and here are a few things to watch out for:

Never pour a wine with the left hand, because that curses the drinker.

Never pour a bottle with the palm up, for that is an insult to the one for whom it is poured.

Never let the neck of the bottle touch the glass, for that puts a curse on the wine.

Never let a glass ting, because that means a sailor has fallen overboard. If the ting is stopped before it fades, the drowning sailor has been saved.

Never let a glass stand empty before the bottle is, because that puts a curse on the company as well as on the house. Some wine must be poured even for those not drinking; to refuse any wine at all is to bring bad luck to all present.

Even when a wine is decanted, the bottle should be left so that the company can see what the wine is. (No consequences result from removing the bottle, so this may really be a custom.)

——————— *THE CALENDAR OF REVELS* ———————

Pagan rites and lore of old religions are holidays for children now or celebrations of the season or feast days, times of revelry more than worship, the Maypole, the pumpkin, and Mardi Gras heralding ancient festivities not quite forgot. While the vineyard calendar begins on St. Vincent's day, January 22, when the year's labor with the vine begins, and

---

——THE BEST SEASONS FOR VARIOUS CHEESES——

Fall through spring/*Pont l'Evèque, Tomme*

First frost to last/*Brie, Coulommiers*

First frost to summer/*Reblochon, Neufchâtel, St. Nectaire*

November through April/*Carre de l'Est, Cantal, Fourme, Roquefort, Bleu, Muenster, Mont d'Or*

November through spring/*Camembert, Epoisses, Vacherin, Maroilles, Livarot*

All year/*Gruyère, Emmenthal, Comté, Beaufort, Port du Salut, St. Paulin, Morbier, St. Rémy*

Spring to New Year/*St. Marcellin, Chabichou*

May to November/*Ste. Maure, Banon, Rigotte de Contrieu*

May to New Year/*Valencay, Persillé, Crottin de Chavignol*

---

the vintner may celebrate the vintage on Michaelmas, September 29, the reveler's calendar for wine more truly begins on the eleventh day of the eleventh month, eleven days before the beginning of winter.*

● *11 November* Martinmas. The day the new wine is first drunk. Martin of Tours, the knight who shared his cloak with a beggar is the patron saint of innkeepers, wine merchants and coopers, among others; he is invoked against drunkenness, storm, and ulcers. In Portugal the first roast chestnuts are eaten with the new wine, in northern Europe there are feasts of sausages, and in England beef or mutton was hung in the chimney to smoke into ham or bacon for the coming winter.

*From Observations on the Popular Antiquities, London, 1848.

● *25 December* Christmas. Bacchanalia and Saturnalia, celebrated at the time of the winter solstice, have become more or less absorbed into the holiday festivities, along with mumming, when men and women exchanged clothes, and danced and sang to their neighbors, their reward a drink from the wassail bowl. Snapdragon is a Yuletide game; raisins on a platter are set aflame with brandy to be snatched and eaten while still flaming to bring luck for all the year. The Yule log is lit, to burn until Twelfthnight, candles are lit for the Feast of Lights; flaming plum puddings decked with holly crown the merriment.

● *1 January* New Year and its Eve. Druidic rites with mistletoe and the crowning of the Lord of Misrule with oak leaf wreaths have been pretty much absorbed into celebrations for the New Year. Champagne corks are popped at midnight, punch bowls are kept filled to brimming, white wine and white sausages are devoured until dawn. Wassailing continues to Twelfthnight; trees in the orchards are beaten with sticks to ensure a good harvest. In Scotland, much attention is paid the wind:

> *If New Year's Eve night-wind blow south,*
> *It betokeneth warmth and growth;*
> *If west, much milk, and fish in the sea;*
> *If north, much cold and storms there will be;*
> *If east, the trees will bear much fruit;*
> *If north-east, flee it man and brute.*

An orange stuck with cloves is a New Year's gift; if one is hung above the wine, it "wyll be preserved from foystiness and evyll savor," according to a footnote to an eighteenth-century edition of Shakespeare, which also recommends "a gift nutmeg." In Paris, the Festival of Fools was once held; in Scotland children once begged for Nog-money but usually got Hogmanay cake made of oatmeal.

● *6 January* Twelfthnight, the last day of Christmas, Feast of the Epiphany. When the King of the Bean is crowned in France—the one who has found the bean in a slice of cake is crowned king—all drink to his health, and the king pays.

● *21 January* St. Agnes' Day and Eve. A day for virgins. The Eve for hope.

● *2 February* Candlemas Day, in honor of the Virgin, when candles are lit to bring good crops and fortune. The Scots forbode, "If Candlemas is fair and clear, there'll be two winters in the year," which is bad for wine.

● *14 February* Valentine's Day. "Birds chase their mates, and couple too, this day," says Herrick, while youth and virgins express their love. Love knots and cards of hearts are given, but especially wine, red and brimming in a loving cup.

● *Mardi Gras* Shrove Tuesday follows Collop Monday, the days of feasting before the fasting of Lent. Pancake day in England. Bacchic Feasts once celebrated in Rome are now revels everywhere. Fasching in Germany, when all rules are suspended.

● *1 April* All Fool's Day. The trick is to send people off on fool's errands. The eighth day after March 25, when spring bacchanalia were celebrated for a week and a day, the octave ending when all were exhausted. Now best celebrated with a toast of wine, to spring.

● *1 May* May Day. After midnight, men and maids would go a-maying, festooning themselves with wreaths and crowns of flowers, with much wining and wooing. There was a Maypole for the children, originally a dance for virgins, and Morris dancing for ten men, often with swords, in honor of Maid Marion and her court of virgins. A time for May wine.

● *21 June* Midsummer Eve. The pagan rite of the summer solstice, counterpart of Yuletide. References to it are in Shakespeare. Also a time of bonfires and cavorting out of doors, with white wine in the loving cups.

● *29 September* Michaelmas. Feast of the archangel who opposed Lucifer. Season of mists and mellow fruitfulness, vintage time, celebrated by gathering fruits and drinking fresh juice. Feasting on the Michaelmas goose after harvest home, to bring good fortune.

●*1 November* Hallowmas, All Hallow's Eve—the witch's New Year. Nutcracker Night is a time for cracking nuts and bobbing for apples. The hallow fire was kindled by the Druids to ward off demons and black witches, and one wears garments of single hue so that vibrations will be good. Old wines are drunk.

────── *THE VINTAGE YEAR/A VINTNER'S CALENDAR* ──────

	Vineyard	Cellar	Tasting
Jan	Pruning, grubbing, new cuttings	First racking	New wines
Feb	Pruning, ploughing, replanting, fertilizing	Second racking	Older cask wines
Mar	Pruning, tying vines	Filtering, bottling	Oldest cask wines
Apr	Setting new vines, tilling, tending	Bottling	New and old wines
May	Fighting frost and fungi, planting, training vines	Treating wines	Old and new wines
June	Spraying, tilling	Tending wines	Cask and bottle wines
July	Spraying, hoeing	Tending wines	Cask and bottle wines
Aug	Spraying, hoeing	Tending wines	Cask and bottle wines
Sep	Scaring birds, vintaging	Preparing casks	Juice and must
Oct	Picking and pressing	Vinification	New wines
Nov	Gleaning, clearing	Tending fermentation	New wines
Dec	Pruning, grubbing	Racking	New and cask wines

7.
Touring the Wine Country

TASTING AT THE SOURCE

Tasting wines in chilly cellars is not the best fun to be had, nor is sampling spoonfuls of wine in tasting rooms. A little goes much too far; half an hour is enough for the most zealous. The best time for tasting wines is during the end of winter, just before spring, when the weather is miserable but winemakers have some time to talk about their wines. Vintage time is the most beautiful in any wine country, but then there is no time for visitors.

Nevertheless, the classic wine tour starts with a day or so in Paris, followed by a couple of days in Champagne, a week in Burgundy, a week along the Rhône, and a week of rest and recovery along the Riviera. You then drive across southern France for a week in Bordeaux, followed by a week along the Loire, with side trips to Armagnac and Cognac along the way, ending up with a week of rest in Paris. Or you can do it in reverse order.

A trip along the Rhine begins in Alsace, with a stopover in Strasbourg, followed by a week in the Rheinpfalz, Rheinhessen, and Rheingau, ending up in Rudesheim for a long night of drinking in the Drosselgasse in Thrush Alley, a tourist trap, and delightful. The wines get sweeter and sweeter, the rinkydink music gets louder and louder, and you link arms with students, locals, and tourists and sing your head off. This is followed by a week on the Mosel. Or you can do that in reverse too.

The best way of all is to pick up whatever wine country comes your way in the course of a vacation. Some of it is enchanting, but vineyards are vineyards. Some of the most beautiful of them are listed below:

● *Vouvray* Along the Loire, near Tours, surrounded by Château country in the smile of France. Caves for storing the wine are dug deep into hillsides. There is also Chinon, sleepy side valleys ...

● *Cognac* A strange country near the sea, with amethyst skies, and amazing distilleries to walk through ... and Cognac.

● *Saint Emilion* A way station for pilgrims on the way to Spain, with Roman ruins atop the hills, a town square with a church beneath, and vineyards rolling down to a winding river—wine country at its best.

● *Armagnac* A part of old France few people ever see, towns that are bastions, with houses overhanging the squares ... and Armagnac.

● *Cassis* Near Marseilles, everyone's idea of a small fishing village, with vineyards climbing to the sky and a corny legend you must hear.

● *Volnay* Beaune has its Hospices and its Roman wall, but the sandy clumps of Volnay houses stuck on a slope too steep for vines, the place of hidden springs, is a town of laughter. You can take the wine road through the famous vineyards.

———*FRENCH REGIONALS, STILL GOOD BUYS?*———

The French have the most sophisticated of control laws, AOC for Appellation d'Origine Contrôlée, *which protect the name of the top 20 percent of French wines—and these are the ones America has become accustomed to buying. The least of these bear regional names, such as Beaujolais and Bordeaux, and many of these are worth sampling; they are undistinguished wines but many of them are dry and drinkable. A sea of others, sold by brand names that sometimes bear AOC identification, can be fair buys, wines that taste good with simple foods.*

　　REDS
　　Brands: Mouton Cadet, B & G Prince Noir, de Luze
　　　　Club Claret, Ecu Royale Claret, Sichel's My Cousin's
　　　　Claret
　　Bourgogne Rouge
　　Côtes-du-Rhône
　　Bordeaux and Bordeaux Supérieur
　　Beaujolais and Beaujolais Supérieur
　　WHITES
　　Brands: Soleil Blanc, Pavillon Blanc
　　Blanc de Blancs
　　Bourgogne Blanc
　　Bordeaux Blanc
　　Muscadet

NOTE: Many of these cost $4 and more, value depending on the shipper and your taste.

●*Alsace* Riquewihr is a medieval village full of life and wine. And food and alcool blanc (strong fruit distillates). There are a hundred such towns going north on the Weinstrasse through the Rheinpfalz and Rheinhessen, but Riquewihr will save you the trip.

● *Bernkastel* The Mosel is wild with apple blossoms in May, sleepy under the steepest vineyards most of the time, a tumble of gray stone, but in September the fountains flow with wine.

● *Florence* Forget the vineyards, drink Chianti in the town. And when you tire, if you do, go to Siena. The land between is full of Chianti vineyards.

────────────── WINE FESTIVALS ──────────────

There are festivals all over Europe, beginning in May and ending with Les Trois Glorieuses in Beaune the third week in November, when *cuvées* donated to the Hospices de Beaune are auctioned off on the Sunday, preceded and followed by crowded, fabulous banquets. There are some 400 festivals along the Rhine, more than a hundred in France, dozens elsewhere. Here is a list of some of the biggest and best:

	France	*Germany*	*Elsewhere*
May	Macon	Deidesheim, Rheinpfalz	
June	Beaune, Saint Emilion	Mittelheim, Rheingau	
July	Alsace	Eltville, Rheingau	Daphne (near Athens)
Aug	Alsace	Wiesloch, Baden	Burgenland (Austria)
Sep	Tours, Dijon, Arbois, Saint Emilion, Chinon, Chablis	Winningen, Mosel, Bernkastel, Mosel	Soave Jerez (Spain) Logroño (Spain)
Oct	Alsace, Beaujolais		Siena, Verona, Asti, Florence
Nov	Beaujolais, Fleurie, Villefranche		

NOTE: National tourist offices can provide dates and places for many other festivals, particularly if you provide an itinerary.

───────────── *BORDEAUX RESTAURANTS* ─────────────

Bordeaux has a multitude of fine restaurants, the full range of the type of eating places that spring up in Paris every year or so, sleek or cushioned. However, turn-of-the-century bistros, cafes of the Twenties, and neighborhood *zincs* serve good omelets, sandwiches, and steaks at modest prices; the patés, salads, bread, and cheeses, are as satisfactory as the carafe wines.

The fancy restaurant in town is Chapon Fin, full of mirrors and greenery, with emphasis on seasonal dishes.

The most fashionable restaurant is the St. James, popular with the younger crowd of Bordelais winemakers and growers, where specialties and classic dishes are served in a panelled room upstairs at tables set far apart so that talk over excellent wines remains private.

A tiny restaurant featuring duck and regional dishes, with a glorious wine list and a selection of some 50 Armagnacs, is La Tupina.

Enthusiasts of "new" cooking can find excellent examples at Le Rouzic, which also has regional specialties for those who want to concentrate on the wines, in a room with dark walls and lots of orchids.

Don't ignore the restaurants in the hotels, particularly the Frantel, and those that cluster around the station. Bordeaux is famous for charcuterie, and a drive through the vineyard towns, where you can pick up some paté, bread, and cheese to eat beside the road, may be the most satisfying way of all to enjoy this center of the world of wines.

──────────── *BURGUNDY RESTAURANTS* ────────────

Burgundy is a vinous wonder and its capitol of Beaune still looks medieval here and there, with its ancient walls, now full of wine cellars. However, grand restaurants are few. Travelers go south to Lyon and environs or get a late start from Paris and dine in Dijon or places in between. By doing so, they miss the Hotel de la Poste, where buyers and shippers have dined together for generations, and they miss Lemellois in Chagny, a temple of good food. Both have splendid collections of Burgundies. Elsewhere, in the many bistros and *pensions* on the various squares and in the side streets, you may have trouble finding much more than a shipper's brand of Beaujolais.

Every place has a few choice bottles available for the asking, though, and with cheese and bread you can make a good meal. More delightful is to buy cheese, paté, and bread in town, buy a bottle or so in one of the shops or on a visit to a wine cellar, then drive out along the vineyard roads. On top of the Golden Slope you will find dozens of places to picnic, looking over some of the most extraordinary wine land on earth.

The wonder of the place is not only the wine, but of being where generations have concerned themselves with the good life and with excellence. Burgundy has a feeling all its own. Maybe you have to be there.

NOTE: Arrangements to visit cellars are best made ahead of time by writing; get the addresses from your favorite labels. You can also make local inquiries, however. The Comité des Vins de la Côte d'Or is in Beaune, Petite Place Carnot. A tour of southern Burgundy, particularly the Beaujolais, offers countless tasting of wines that should be drunk on the spot. For information, try Beaujolais Union des Vins, 24 Boulevard Vermorel in Ville-franche, or the Comité des Vins de Bourgogne, in Mâcon at 3 bis rue Gambetta.

> *Machine production of food and drink, like machine production of other things, gives us something slick and sterile; hygienic methods, admirable though they are, remove not only imperfections, but virtues. In all crafts, whether the making of wine or beer, the making of clothes, the making of furniture or bread or pastry, you must, for vitality and character, have the touch of the living human hand. ... The man who held that there was no such thing as bad liquor—it was only that some was better than others—should have lived to taste some of the concoctions of these days....*
>
> *Speaking of wine—I mean real wine—a welcome addition to the London scene would be a group of wine bars which covered the whole wine list. The majority of wine bars seem to limit themselves to sherry, port, Madeira and champagne. At only a few places can one call for a little Niersteiner or Zeltinger, a glass of good Bordeaux, of Chianti or Capri. The wines of France and Germany of course present the difficulty that a bottle once opened is useless the next day.*
>
> Will Someone Lead Me to a Pub?*
> *Thomas Burke (1886-1945)*

——— *VIENNA'S HEURIGEN ... mit Schrammel* ———

Soon after vintage the papers publish lists of which heurige houses are hanging out the bush, and the Viennese catch trolley number 38 at the Schottenring and ride out to Grinzing, the end of the line. There are gardens with tables under trellises and timbered inns on both sides of the cobbled streets, the deedle of concertinas backed by guitars and a brace of fiddles, the smell of baked bread, sizzling sausages, roast chickens—and new wine.

*From The Flowing Bowl, Geoffrey Mortlock and Stephen Williams. Reprinted by permission of Routledge and Kegan Paul, Ltd.

There are the opera and the coffee houses, the Prater and its Ferris wheel, pastry shops and Schönbrunn and the Spanish Riding School, but especially there is the Grinzing. You drink *viertels*—quarter liters—of the sprightly, soft but sharp, sometimes cloudy wines made from the Veltliner, water-white and tinged with gold. Some heurigen open for lunch, but afternoons are better, and evenings, far into the night.

The wines come not only from Grinzing, but several towns around the countryside. One can try to sample them all:

Kahlenbergerdorf	Heiligenstadt
Nussdorf	Sievering
Unterdöbling	Neustift

But there are many others, and you can find your own, where the folksy Schrammel music is played as the wine flows. There's always someone to teach you the songs and declaim the saws, like this one:

> Not to say that man may not drink more than needful, and he may well allow himself a little indulgence. That is what wine is for, but nobody should have more than six viertels at once, for temperance is a lovely virtue, most pleasing to the gods.

But be warned. Another saying has it:

> *First glass for thirst*
> *Second for sustenance,*
> *Third for pleasure ...*
> *But the fourth's for madness.*

—— *WINES FOR BOATING, TOURING, CAMPING* ——

Bottles are heavy; they smash easily. Jostling and heat can ruin a wine in a day or so. But lifting a bottle from a brook or holding a glass so that you can see the campfire through the wine are romantic pleasures worth experiencing.

Bottles wrapped in clothing or newspaper, clipped into hampers, or packed in ice will survive a morning's drive or sail. The real problem is glasses; they should be not necessarily stemmed, but clear enough so that you can see the wine. Paper or plastic cups don't change the taste of a wine, but seem to, and metal cups are worst of all. A stack of juice glasses wrapped in newspaper does very well.

The wines should be young and full of taste to compete with the tang of fresh air. Perhaps the best are jug wines—any jug wine—because they are made to have a long shelf life and to be drinkable for hours, once opened. For stowing, the wine is best poured into plastic bottles with screw caps. In small sizes they can be tucked in a pack or wedged into a corner. Champagne bottles should be chilled well, then wrapped in a blanket or other covering that will keep it cool for several hours, and then it should be cooled again before being opened. Wines that travel well include the following:

●*Sherry* Particularly dry Manzanillas and Finos, and nutty Amontillados. Cooled, these wines are marvelous with salads, cold cuts, and sandwiches. Sweet Olorosos are a dessert in themselves.

●*Porto* Ruby and tawny Portos are delicious with melons and with nuts, with bread and jams that are not too sweet, with fruit cake and those without icing. Guava jelly and cream cheese on crackers, with Porto, make a satisfying open-air meal.

●*Riesling* Flowery, usually soft, sometimes fruity and lightly sweet, these wines are refreshing by themselves, with fruit and cheese, with salads that are more than greens, and with fish or seafood, hot or cold. The wine is good when only cool, although better when well chilled.

●*Muscadet and Other Dry Whites* The sharp taste of fresh, dry white wine is particularly good with cheeses that are sliced, with fish and seafood, with cold chicken and cold cuts. It is best when well cooled.

● *Beaujolais* The perfect picnic wine. It's best served cool; chill in the refrigerator, wrap in newspaper, serve within six hours.

● *Champagne* A nuisance. Heavy and bulky, hard to carry, truly good only when very cold—and always worth the effort. The best wine of all for drinking out of doors. Also good in cabins, sailboats, ski lodges, beach houses, tents, third-rate motels. Carry glasses.

● *Chianti, Soave, and Others* Good wines with all sorts of antipasto, although often bland with al fresco foods.

● *Rioja* The driest of red wines generally available, not too full and often light, perhaps the best wine for campfire and barbecue meats, on a par with Beaujolais, but quite different.

NOTE: You can occasionally pick up interesting local wines while touring, although wise travelers generally stick a bottle or two in the trunk before starting off. Slices of pumpernickel rounds spread with cream cheese and slices of salami and cucumber are delicious with all wines.

The jolly god in triumph comes;
Sound the trumpets; beat the drums ...
Bacchus ever fair and young
Drinking joys did first ordain;
Bacchus' blessings are a treasure ...
Rich the treasure;
Sweet the pleasure;
Sweet is pleasure after pain

Scamped from Dryden

Index

Index

Index

Index

Index

Index

Index

Index

Vaillon, 54
Valdepeñas, 28, 128
Valdivieso, 27
Valmont, 27
Valmur, 36, 54
Valpolicella, 31-32, 85, 128
Valtellina, 85, 129
Varietal wines, 91
Varoilles, les, 44
Vaucoupin, 54
Vaucrains, les, 47
Vaudésin, 36, 54
VDPV (Verband Deutscher
    Prädikatswein Versteigerer), 155
VDQS (Vins Délimités de Qualité
    Superiéure), 25, 27, 28, 74, 129,
    153-54
Veneto, 28, 85
Verdicchio, 35, 85, 128
Verdiso, 35, 85
Vergelesses, 50
Vermouth, 149
Verona, 31
Vertical tasting, 137
Vienna, 205-6
Vineyards, leading French and
    German, 35-37
Vinho Verde, 27
Vino Nobile de Montepluciano, 85
Vintage year, 2-3
Vintages
  big, 10
  old, 130-31
  ratings and rankings, 1-23 *passim*
Viognier, 34, 68
Viticulteur, 14
Vogros, 54
Volnay, 36, 47, 48, 55, 129, 200
Volnay-Santenots, 55
Vosne-Romanée, 36, 46, 55
Vougeot, 36, 55
Vouvray, 71, 72, 200

VP (Vin du pays), 75-76, 154
VQPRD (Vins de Qualité Produits
    dan des Régions Determinées),
    154
VSOP (Very Superior Old Pale), 155

Wachau, 27
Wachenheimer Mariengarten, 37, 82
Wagner, Philip, 99
Washington, 3, 102
Wehlen Münzlay, 37, 78
Weibel, 91
Wente Bros., 91
West Germany, 38
White Riesling, 22, 30, 34, 83, 129
White wines, 3, 4, 13-15, 34-35, 41,
    85, 146
Wiesbaden, 79
Wiltingener Scharzberg, 37, 78
Wine lists, 114-19
Wine by percent alcohol, 154
Wine terms
  French, 165-70
  German, 170-75
  Italian, 175-77
  Spanish, 178-79
Wine tour, 199-202
Winkeler Honigberg, 80
Wisconsin, 100
Würzburg, 82
Würzgarten, 78

XO (Extra Old), 155

Yago, 26
Yquem, Château, 36
Yugoslavia, 27, 33, 38

Zeltinger Münzlay, 37, 78
Zeus, 181
Zinfandel, 22, 23, 33, 129
Zwicker, 69